世界的宁波
宁波的世界

Ningbo,
A Coastal City
For Global Minds

E 121°32′
N 29°52′

宁波人才发展集团有限公司 编著

中国发展出版社
CHINA DEVELOPMENT PRESS

图书在版编目（CIP）数据

世界的宁波，宁波的世界 / 宁波人才发展集团有限公司编著．—北京：中国发展出版社，2024.3（2024.5 重印）

ISBN 978-7-5177-1416-3

Ⅰ．①世…　Ⅱ．①宁…　Ⅲ．①宁波－概况　Ⅳ．①K925.53

中国国家版本馆 CIP 数据核字（2024）第 071930 号

书　　名：世界的宁波，宁波的世界
著作责任者：宁波人才发展集团有限公司
责 任 编 辑：沈海霞　吴若瑜
出 版 发 行：中国发展出版社
联 系 地 址：北京经济技术开发区荣华中路 22 号亦城财富中心 1 号楼 8 层（100176）
标 准 书 号：ISBN 978-7-5177-1416-3
经　销　者：各地新华书店
印　刷　者：北京博海升彩色印刷有限公司
开　　本：710mm × 1000mm　1/16
印　　张：15
字　　数：274 千字
版　　次：2024 年 3 月第 1 版
印　　次：2024 年 5 月第 2 次印刷
定　　价：88.00 元

联 系 电 话：（010）68990535　68360970
购 书 热 线：（010）68990682　68990686
网 络 订 购：http://zgfzcbs.tmall.com
网 购 电 话：（010）88333349　68990639
本 社 网 址：http://www.develpress.com
电 子 邮 件：174912863@qq.com

本书编委会

致谢单位

中共宁波市委组织部
中共宁波市委宣传部
中共宁波市委统一战线工作部
中共宁波市委社会工作部
中共宁波市委政法委员会
宁波市发展和改革委员会
宁波市经济和信息化局
宁波市教育局
宁波市科学技术局
宁波市公安局
宁波市人力资源和社会保障局
宁波市住房和城乡建设局
宁波市交通运输局
宁波市水利局
宁波市农业农村局
宁波市商务局
宁波市文化广电旅游局
宁波市卫生健康委员会
宁波市人民政府外事办公室
宁波市人民政府国有资产监督管理委员会
宁波市市场监督管理局
宁波市体育局
宁波市统计局
宁波市投资促进局
中国共产主义青年团宁波市委员会
宁波市科学技术协会
宁波东海经济研究院
宁波大学中东欧经贸合作研究院
宁波市博纳资讯传播有限公司

The Editorial Committee

Special Gratitude To

the Organization Department of the CPC Ningbo Municipal Committee

the Publicity Department of the CPC Ningbo Municipal Committee

United Front Work Department, CPC Ningbo Municipal Committee

Social Work Department of the CPC Ningbo Municipal Committee

Political and Legal Affairs Commission of the CPC Ningbo Municipal Committee

Ningbo Municipal Development & Reform Commission

Ningbo Municipal Economic and Information Technology Bureau

Ningbo Education Bureau

Ningbo Science and Technology Bureau

Ningbo Public Security Bureau

Ningbo Municipal Human Resources and Social Security Bureau

Ningbo Housing and Urban-Rural Development Bureau

Ningbo Municipal Transport Bureau

Ningbo Water Resources Bureau

Ningbo Agricultural and Rural Bureau

Ningbo Municipal Bureau of Commerce

Ningbo Municipal Bureau of Culture, Radio, Television and Tourism

Health Commission of Ningbo

Ningbo Municipal Foreign Affairs Office

State-owned Assets Supervision and Administration Commission of Ningbo Municipal Government

Ningbo Municipal Administration for Market Regulation

Ningbo Sports Bureau

Ningbo Municipal Statistics Bureau

Ningbo Investment Promotion Bureau

Ningbo Committee of the Chinese Communist Youth League

Ningbo Association of Science and Technology

Ningbo Donghai Economic Research Institute

Institute of China-CEEC Economic and Trade Cooperation, Ningbo University

Ningbo Bona Media Co., Ltd.

海定波宁，活力奔“甬”

Ningbo: A Start-Up Powerhouse

泱泱东方大港，浩浩八面来风。招揽九天日月，吞吐五洲风云。“宁波”之名，源于“海定则波宁”。它，诠释着这座城市的幸福厚度、幸福态度、幸福纯度和幸福气度。

In the Oriental harbor grand and wide, winds whisper tales from every side. Celestial lights enchant the scene, a world of wonder, forever keen. Cultures meet as ships arrive, a melting pot where dreams survive. This harbor, where stories unfurl, witness to wonders, in every whirl.

The name "Ningbo" originates from the saying "If the sea is settled, the waves are peaceful". It tells of the city's profundity, attitude, purity and temperament.

“海”——幸福厚度

City of Strength by the Sea

宁波因海而生、凭海而兴、向海图强，地处中国东海之滨、长江三角洲南翼，东濒舟山，西接绍兴，北枕杭州湾，南扼台（台州）温（温州）闽（福建）。

Ningbo, a coastal city nestled along the East China Sea, has flourished and expanded under the constant sway of its maritime heritage. It lies in the southern wing of the Yangtze River Delta, flanked by Zhoushan Archipelago to the east, Shaoxing to the west, Hangzhou Bay to the north, and Taizhou, Wenzhou and Fujian to the south.

港口是宁波最大的资源，开放是宁波最大的优势，只有把最大资源和最大优势发挥到极致，才能实现效益最大化。

Ports serve as the most valuable asset, and openness its principal strength. By capitalizing on this crucial asset and strength, the city can optimize its benefits to the maximum degree.

站在服务国家战略的前沿，宁波在全球战略视野下找准发展的新的历史方位，牢记“国之大者”，加快建设现代化滨海大都市，彰显应有的实力和使命担当。

Ningbo positions itself at the vanguard of national development, embracing a renewed historical responsibility within a global strategic vision. Committed to the pursuit of national greatness, the city is hastening the construction of a modern coastal metropolis, unveiling its innate potential and realizing its pivotal role.

锻强硬核实力。2023 年宁波市实现地区生产总值约 1.65 万亿元，稳居全国城市第 12 位。今日宁波以全国 1‰的土地面积、1/150 的人口，贡献着全国约 1/60 的国内生产总值、1/20 的进出口总额……

An economic powerhouse. In 2023, Ningbo's GDP attained 1.65 trillion yuan, ranking it as the 12th largest nationwide. Ningbo's contribution to the national economy is notable. With just 1 ‰ of the land area and 1/150th of the population, the city accounts for approximately 1/60th of the GDP and 1/20th of the total import and export volume of China.

开放海港口岸。宁波与全球 220 多个国家和地区直接进行贸易往来，成为全国第六座“外贸万亿之城”，中国－中东欧国家经贸合作示范区成为共建“一带一路”的“金名片”。

Gateway to the world. Ningbo, boasting direct trade links with over 220 countries, has secured its status as China's sixth trillion city in foreign trade. The establishment of the China-Central and Eastern European Countries (CEEC) Business Cooperation Demonstration Zone has further bolstered Ningbo's position as a pivotal hub in the "Belt and Road", symbolizing its notable achievements.

打造世界强港。2023 年宁波舟山港货物吞吐量超 13.24 亿吨，连续 15 年居于世界首位；集装箱吞吐量连续 6 年位居世界第三，成为国家战略中的“硬核力量”。

A world-class port. In 2023, Ningbo Zhoushan Port maintained its position as the world's premier port for 15 consecutive years, handling an annual cargo throughput of over 1.324 billion tons. Its container throughput also ranked third globally for the sixth year running. These impressive achievements underscore the port's crucial contribution to the national strategy and its importance in the global trade.

升级“宁波智造”。宁波有国家级制造业单项冠军企业 104 家，居全国城市首位；国家级专精特新“小巨人”企业 352 家，居全国城市第四位；加速形成 3 个万亿级产业集群及 6 个千亿级产业集群，展现了新型工业化的勃勃生机。

City of smart manufacturing. Ningbo proudly hosts 104 state-level manufacturing champion enterprises, securing its leading status nationwide. It also boasts 352 state-level specialized high-growth "Little Giant" enterprises, claiming the fourth spot in the national ranking. Additionally, the city is rapidly establishing three trillion-yuan-level industrial clusters and six hundred-billion-yuan-level industrial clusters, showcasing the dynamism of new industrialization.

“定”——幸福态度
City of Courtesy

宁波是一座让人来了就不想走的城市。在这里，生活很安心、发展很顺心、感受很暖心，市民有自豪感、归属感、安全感。

Ningbo is a city that delivers greatest wellbeing to its residents. Here, life unfolds peacefully amidst thriving development, while the community exudes a welcoming warmth. Its residents share a profound sense of pride, belonging, and security.

气定，源自口袋富足。2023 年，宁波城乡居民人均可支配收入分别超 8 万元、4.8 万元，城乡居民人均收入倍差降至 1.66，连续 20 年呈缩小态势，在全国名列前茅，共同富裕真实可感。

Ningbo is a city of abundance. In 2023, it witnessed significant progress in income equality, with the per capita disposable income of urban residents surpassing 80000 yuan and that of rural residents exceeding 48000 yuan. The income gap between urban and rural areas has been consistently narrowing for the past 20 years, reflecting tangible improvements in common prosperity.

气定，源自文明有礼。宁波蝉联全国文明城市之列，成为首批文明典范城市试点；全民阅读、礼让斑马线成为风尚；涌现出一大批道德典型，崇德向善蔚然成风。

Ningbo is a city of civility. It has proudly earned the prestigious title of a National Civilized City for six years running. This accolade cements the status of this coastal city as a vanguard among the pioneering pilot cities for promoting civility. Reading has emerged as a popular trend for all, while yielding to crosswalks has become a fashionable norm. The city has also witnessed a surge in individuals recognized as morality models, fostering a trend that advocates for morality and goodness.

气定，源自和谐治理。宁波入选了全国市域社会治理现代化试点。在宁波，办事办证有“最多跑一次”服务，基层自治有“村民说事”制度，社会智治有“移动微法院”。

Ningbo is a city of harmonious governance. It has been selected as a national pilot for modernizing social governance. If in need of administrative affairs to be done and licensing to be approved by authorities, you only need to visit the related administrative departments once. Villagers' self-governance is practiced and "Mobile Micro-courts" are in place within communities.

“波”——幸福纯度
City of Superb Environment

“四明八百里，物色甲东南”。行走在宁波大地上，举目皆是青山绿水、诗画江南的美景。“在宁波，都挺好”成为市民的共同观感。

Spanning thousands of square kilometers, Ningbo is renowned for its vast ecological diversity and exceptional environment. Journeying through the city's extensive reaches, every view presents lush mountains and glistening waters, reflecting the picturesque charm of a Jiangnan-style landscape (in the region south of the Yangtze River). The phrase "Everything in Ningbo is superb" has become a common sentiment among its inhabitants.

都挺好，好在生态环境。全域建设大美宁波，实施蓝天、碧水、净土、清废行动，成为国家级生态文明建设先行示范区。绿色已成为宁波的幸福底色。

The ecological environment is superb. By turning the entire city into a stunning landscape, Ningbo has been taking strides in ensuring clear skies, clean waters, uncontaminated land, and effective waste management. It serves as a pioneering model, trailblazing as a demonstration zone for constructing national-level ecological civilization. Green has emerged as the foundational hue of happiness in Ningbo.

都挺好，好在人居环境。宁波率先提出打造“最干净城市”“席地而坐之城”的目标，让枕山面海、拥江揽湖的大都市魅力竞相绽放。

The living environment is superb. Ningbo has taken the lead in building "the cleanest city" and zones of "sitting on the ground". It unfurls its metropolitan charm, nestled between mountains and sea, embracing rivers and lakes within its grasp.

都挺好，好在营商环境。宁波以数字化改革推动政务服务转型，建成“无证件办事之城”“掌上办事之市”，获评全国营商环境标杆城市。

The business environment is superb. Through digital innovation, Ningbo has revolutionized its administrative services, establishing itself as a documents-free zone and a hub for accessible services at your fingertips. This has helped Ningbo gain national acclaim as a standard-setting city for top-notch business environments.

都挺好，好在服务环境。立足人的全生命周期需求，宁波全力打造七个“浙里甬有”幸福民生品牌，优质共享公共服务，擦亮中国“最具幸福感城市”金字招牌。

The service environment is superb. Concentrating on the needs that span the entire spectrum of an individual's life, Ningbo is dedicated to crafting seven distinct brands of livelihood service. By providing high-quality, shared public services, the city is burnishing its golden reputation as China's "happiest city".

“宁”——幸福气度

City of Profound Culture

书藏古今，宁静致远。深厚的文化底蕴，让宁波多了一份创造幸福、感受幸福的自信与从容。

Ningbo is a city of culture and serenity. Its deep cultural roots instill a sense of poise and elegance in both the creation and enjoyment of happiness.

这里有赓续千年的文脉流长。约 8300 年前的河姆渡文化井头山遗址，见证了中华海洋文明的起源；亚洲最古老的藏书楼天一阁，树立起甬城的精神地标；王阳明、黄宗羲等先贤蜚声海内外，122 位甬籍院士让“院士之乡”的美誉声名远播。

It boasts a cultural lineage that has continued for thousands of years. The Jingtoushan site of the Hemudu Culture, dating back 8300 years, bears witness to the origin of Chinese maritime civilization. Tianyige Library (aka. Tianyi Pavilion), the oldest existing library in Asia, stands as a cultural landmark of Ningbo. Esteemed sages like Wang Yangming and Huang Zongxi have earned accolades far and wide, while the 122 academicians hailing from Ningbo let the reputation of the "Hometown of Academicians" resonate broadly.

这里有知行合一的务实气质。宁波人亦文亦武，文是院士，武是商家，文武相济，大事必成。邓小平同志“把全世界的‘宁波帮’都动员起来建设宁波”的倡议提出 40 年来，新时代“宁波帮”兴起实干兴邦的热潮，从宁波日益走近世界舞台中央。

It thrives on a pragmatic ethos of unity between knowledge and action. "The people of Ningbo are both scholarly and martial. Ningbo nurtures both academicians and entrepreneurs. With the combined strengths of intellect and commerce, great things are surely to be achieved." Since Deng Xiaoping's directive 40 years ago to "engage the ‘Ningbo Native Merchants' (known as "Ning Bo Bang" in Chinese pinyin) worldwide in developing Ningbo," the modern-day Ningbo Native Merchants have ignited a fervor of progressive diligence towards national prosperity, continually elevating Ningbo to an increasingly prominent position on the global stage.

这里有自觉自信的文化先行。宁波首创“艺术振兴乡村”模式，“一人一艺”全民艺术普及，诗和远方就在市民的身边。“东亚文化之都”搭起文明交流的桥梁，让海上丝绸之路“活化石”继续扬帆世界。

It instantiates the spearheading of culture with conscious confidence. Ningbo has pioneered a model of "rural revitalization through art" to make the beauty of art readily accessible to the general public. As the "Cultural Capital of East Asia", the city serves as a conduit for cultural interactions, propelling the "living fossil" of the Maritime Silk Road to continually embark on its journey across the global stage.

这里有海纳百川的爱才环境。栽下梧桐树，引得凤凰来。宁波和你同频共振，汇八方英才，谱盛世华章。

It features highly favorable policies to attract talented individuals. Welcome to Ningbo, where dreams find their wings and aspirations take flight. This vibrant city embraces you with open arms, offering endless possibilities and a nurturing environment to turn your dreams into reality.

来吧！无论你是初生牛犊不怕虎的“后浪”、弄潮儿向涛头立的天之骄子，还是担当中流砥柱的业界精英，活力宁波，等你奔“甬”而来！

Come and join us! Regardless of whether you are a fearless calf unafraid of tigers, a proud trailblazer leading the charge, or an accomplished industry elite, the lively city of Ningbo eagerly awaits your arrival.

目 录 | Contents

篇章一
Chapter One

滨海宁波，闪耀未来
Ningbo, A Promising Port City

篇章二
Chapter Two

奔“甬”而来，凤凰筑巢
Hub of Brains and Start-ups

篇章三
Chapter Three

都市乐活，人间烟火
City of True Happiness

篇章一
Chapter One

滨海宁波，闪耀未来
Ningbo, A Promising Port City

宁波东部新城　Ningbo Eastern New Town

宁波是一座向海而生、向海图强的城市，正如它的名字一般，宁静和波澜此起彼伏。

Ningbo, a city by the East China Sea, thrives with vibrant waves.

回首过去，宁波以独特的资源禀赋和深厚的历史底蕴，塑造了开放大气的城市特色。

With its rich resources and profound historical heritage, this coastal city has

cultivated an open and vibrant atmosphere that makes it stand out among all cities in China.

面向未来，宁波擘画新蓝图，以更高的标准、更大的气魄、更宽的视野、更高的品位，全面建设现代化滨海大都市，谱写新的时代传奇。

Ningbo has unveiled a blueprint for the construction of a modern coastal metropolis with higher standards, bolder vision, and broader horizons.

速览城市名片
City Profile

宁波市中心　Bird's-eye view of downtown Ningbo

宁波市夜景　Night view of downtown Ningbo

宁波，简称“甬”，取“海定则波宁”之义。宁波地处中国东南沿海，是一座位于北纬30°线上的现代化滨海大都市。

Ningbo, "Yong" for short, takes its name from the saying "If the sea is calm, the waves are peaceful". Situated on the southeastern coast of China, Ningbo stands proudly as a modern coastal metropolis bustling on the 30th parallel of north latitude.

这里以水为魂，倚港衍生，既有江南水乡的诗情画意，也有海港城市的锐意进取，以“书藏古今，港通天下”的城市名片享誉全球。

With water as its soul and its port as its source, Ningbo exudes the enchanting ambiance typical of Jiangnan water regions, complemented by the enterprising spirit of a thriving seaport city. Renowned globally as the "City of Culture and Gateway to the World," it showcases its unique identity to the world.

宁波是计划单列市，是长江三角洲南翼经济中心，综合经济实力在中国各城市中位于第 12 名[①]。

Ningbo, a city individually listed in the national economic plan, stands as the economic powerhouse in the southern wing of the Yangtze River Delta. It holds the 12th position in China, evidencing its robust comprehensive economic strength[①].

背靠中国大陆，面向东海，宁波与生俱来的海纳百川、开放包容的胸襟魅力，也孕育了勇立潮头、开拓进取的宁波人。

Ningbo, nestled against the Chinese mainland and facing the East China Sea, possesses an innate charm of embracing diverse cultures and an open-minded spirit. This dynamic city has nurtured visionary individuals who fearlessly lead the way and embrace new horizons.

自然地理。宁波的坐标为东经 120° 55′ 至 122° 16′，北纬 28° 51′ 至 30° 33′，位于中国大陆海岸线中段、长江三角洲南翼，东有舟山群岛为天然屏障，北濒杭州湾，西接绍兴市，南邻台州市，与美国休斯敦、新奥尔良，埃及开罗，印度新德里等城市同处神秘的北纬 30°。

Geographical Location. Ningbo (120° 55′—122° 16′E and 28° 51′—30° 33′N) lies in the middle section of the Chinese mainland coast and on the southern wing of the Yangtze River Delta. It is bordered by the Zhoushan Archipelago to the east, the Hangzhou Bay to the north, Shaoxing City to the west, and Taizhou City to the south. Additionally, Ningbo shares the mysterious latitude north of 30° with cities like Cairo, Delhi, Houston, and New Orleans.

宁波地势西南高、东北低，以平原丘陵为主，甬江水系穿城而过。全市陆域面积 9816 平方千米，略大于美国纽约、加拿大多伦多等城市。海域面积 8355.8 平方千米，拥有绵延的岸线、多样的海岛、优美的海湾。宁波属于典型的北亚热带季风气候，温和湿润、雨量充沛，四季较为分明。

---

① 资料来源：2023 年各城市国民经济和社会发展统计公报。
Source: 2023 Statistics Bulletin of National Economy and Social Development of Chinese Cities

The topography of Ningbo displays a dramatic variation, with higher elevations in the southwest gradually descending to lower areas in the northeast. The region is predominantly characterized by plains and hills, with the Yong River flowing through the city, enriching its water system. Ningbo is 9816 km^2 in land area, slightly larger than cities like New York in the United States and Toronto in Canada. With a maritime area of 8355.8 km^2, it boasts a picturesque coastline, diverse islands, and beautiful bays. There is a typical North Subtropical Monsoon climate, characterized by mild and humid conditions, ample rainfall, and clearly defined four seasons.

区划人口。宁波市下辖 6 个区、2 个县和 2 个县级市，分别是海曙区、江北区、镇海区、北仑区、鄞州区、奉化区、宁海县、象山县、余姚市、慈溪市。截至 2023 年，宁波常住人口接近 1000 万人，与匈牙利人口相当。城镇化率接近 80%，中心城区人口近 370 万人[②]，是中国 I 型大城市，接近发达国家城市化水平。

Districts and Population. Ningbo is composed of six districts, two counties, and two county-level cities. The districts include Haishu, Jiangbei, Zhenhai, Beilun, Yinzhou, and Fenghua. The counties consist of Ninghai and Xiangshan, while the county-level cities include Yuyao and Cixi. By the end of 2023, the population of Ningbo ran close to 10 million, a figure comparable to the entire population of Hungary. With an impressive urbanization rate of 80% and an urban population nearing 3.7 million[②], Ningbo ranks among China's Tier-1 cities, approaching urbanization levels typically seen in developed countries.

经济发展。2023 年，宁波实现地区生产总值 16452.8 亿元（折合约 2334.8 亿美元），居中国城市第 12 位，接近卡塔尔、新西兰等国家的 GDP 总量。三次产业之比为 2.3∶45.8∶51.9，呈现先进制造业和现代服务业双轮驱动的发展格局。

Economic Development. In 2023, Ningbo achieved a regional gross domestic

② 资料来源：宁波市人民政府官网。
Source: Official website of Ningbo Municipal People's Government.

product of 1645.28 billion yuan (equivalent to approximately 233.48 billion US dollars at the average annual exchange rate). This places Ningbo as the 12th largest city in China, close to the GDP of Qatar or New Zealand. The industrial structure of Ningbo is characterized by a balanced development of the primary, secondary, and tertiary industries. The ratio of these three sectors is 2.3：45.8：51.9, highlighting a robust "double-wheel drive" pattern led by the advanced manufacturing and modern service industries.

宁波藏富于民，按常住人口计算，全市人均地区生产总值逾 17 万元（折合约 25000 美元）③，与中等发达国家葡萄牙在同一水平。

Ningbo, a well-off city, boasts a per capita regional GDP of 170000 yuan (equivalent to approximately 25000 US dollars at the average annual exchange rate) based on its permanent resident population③. This places it on par with upper-middle-income advanced nations like Portugal.

历史沿革。宁波历史悠久，8300 多年前的井头山遗址见证了宁波地区先民迈出向海而生的第一步。7000 多年前，宁波先民创立了河姆渡部落，向世人呈现出饭稻羹鱼、万物有灵的远古江南风情。

History. With a history spanning over thousands of years, Ningbo's journey towards the sea began with the footsteps of our ancestors at the ancient Jingtoushan Ruins, dating back more than 8300 years. Over 7000 years ago, these ancestors established the Hemudu Tribe, revealing to the world the ancient charm of Jiangnan water towns with its cultivation of rice, fishing, and the belief in the spirits within all things.

宁波在夏商时代（约公元前 2070 年—公元前 1046 年）称“鄞”，春秋时（公元前 770 年—公元前 476 年）为越国境地。秦时（公元前 221 年—公元前 206 年）于今境内设鄞、鄮、句章、余姚四县，唐时（618 年—907 年）称“明州”。

③ 资料来源：Top Edb 经济数据智能分析平台。
Source: Top Edb Economic Data Intelligence Analytics Platform.

In the Xia and Shang Dynasties (approximately 2070 BC-1046 BC), Ningbo was known as "Yin", and during the Spring and Autumn Period (770 BC-476 BC), it was part of the Yue State. During the Qin Dynasty (221 BC-206 BC), Ningbo was under the jurisdiction of four counties: Yin, Mao, Gouzhang, and Yuyao. In the Tang Dynasty (618-907), it was known as "Mingzhou".

唐长庆元年（821 年），明州州治迁到三江口（甬江、姚江、奉化江交汇之地）并筑子城，标志着宁波建城之始。明洪武十四年（1381 年），取“海定则波宁”之义改称“宁波”，一直沿用至今。

In 821, the capital of Mingzhou Prefecture was relocated to Sanjiangkou (the confluence of three rivers, i.e., the Yong, Fenghua, and Yuyao rivers), and the construction of fortress and city walls marked the beginning of Ningbo's city establishment. In 1381, the city was officially renamed Ningbo, a name that symbolizes the tranquility of the sea when the waves are calm. This name has endured to the present day.

1987 年，宁波成为计划单列市，具有较大权限制定地方性法规，后被确定为中国 15 个副省级城市之一。

In 1987, Ningbo gained recognition as a separately listed city in the state's economic plan, granting it greater autonomy in implementing local regulations. Seven years later, it was designated as one of China's 15 sub-provincial cities.

文化底蕴。亚洲现存历史最悠久、最古老的私人藏书楼天一阁，享有“南国书城”的盛誉，见证着书香文化的延续和发展；明代哲学家王阳明开创“阳明学派”，以“知行合一”为核心的阳明文化在全世界影响深远；五大佛教名山之一的雪窦山上，端坐着拥有和乐笑容的“人间弥勒”，透露出包容之意；古代明州港（宁波港）江海通航水运航标天封塔，矗立千年，诉说着悠久灿烂的海丝文化。

Profound Culture. Tianyige Library, the oldest surviving private library in Asia, holds the prestigious title of "Book City of South China", showcasing the deep-rooted literary culture and its continuous development. Wang Yangming,

宁波院士中心　Ningbo Academician Center

a renowned philosopher of the Ming Dynasty, established the influential Wang Yangming School, advocating the philosophy of the "unity of knowing and acting" that has resonated globally. Mount Xuedou, one of the five famous Buddhist mountains, features an iconic statue of Maitreya, emanating a serene and joyful expression that embodies the spirit of inclusivity. Mingzhou Port, now known as Ningbo Port, has a rich maritime history, with the Tianfeng Pagoda serving as a symbol of navigation for centuries, reflecting the city's enduring and remarkable legacy in the maritime culture of the Silk Road.

近现代，“宁波帮”叱咤商海，足迹遍布天下，以“无宁不成市”闻名

遐迩，为上海的崛起和香港的繁荣作出了重大贡献。当代，宁波更是著名的“院士之乡”，宁波籍两院院士数量居全国第一位。

In modern times, the Ningbo Native Merchants exert significant influence in the business sphere, extending their reach globally. They have gained prominence for the statement, "A market cannot be formed and business cannot be conducted without people from Ningbo." Their substantial contributions were integral to the rise of Shanghai and the prosperity of Hong Kong. In contemporary times, Ningbo is reputed as the "City of Academicians", recognized for having the highest number of members from Ningbo of the two academies [Chinese Academy of Sciences (CAS) and Chinese Academy of Engineering (CAE)] across the country.

遇见开放港城
An Open Port City

宁波舟山港　Ningbo Zhoushan Port

开放是流淌在宁波城市血液里的基因。

Openness is deeply rooted in the spirit of Ningbo.

从古代“海上丝绸之路”始发港之一，到中国第一批拥有海关的通商城市，再到首批 14 个沿海开放城市之一，宁波向海图强，开放创新。

It served as one of the starting ports of the ancient Maritime Silk Road and secured the status of one of China's earliest cities with customs and commerce. The city subsequently emerged as one of the pioneering 14 coastal cities to embrace openness and has consistently embraced a spirit of progress and openness.

今天，宁波站在一个全新的历史起点上，紧紧依靠宁波舟山港这一最大的资源，牢牢把握“一带一路”这个最大机遇、最大平台，不断谱写开放新篇章。

These days, the city is embarking on an exciting new chapter in its history, propelled by the vast resources of Ningbo Zhoushan Port and a strong commitment to the "Belt and Road" Initiative. Embracing this initiative as its foremost mission, greatest opportunity, and most crucial platform, the city is forging ahead with a dynamic narrative of openness and progress.

（一）港通天下
Gateway to the World

宁波古港，帆樯林立。早在 1000 多年前的唐代，满载丝绸、茶叶、瓷器的船只从宁波出发，驶向蔚蓝海洋，开启了闻名于世的“海上丝绸之路”。

Mingzhou Port has witnessed vibrant maritime activities. As early as 1000 years ago during the Tang Dynasty, ships loaded with silk, tea, and porcelain set sail from Ningbo, embarking on the renowned "Maritime Silk Road" that extended to the far reaches of the blue oceans.

如今，宁波舟山港傲立东方、港通天下，300 多条集装箱航线连接着 200 余个国家和地区的 600 多个港口，货物吞吐量 15 年蝉联全球首位，集装箱吞吐量连续6年位列全球第三[④]，勾画出一张链接全球的海上航运贸易网。

Nowadays, Ningbo Zhoushan Port stands in the East, connecting the world. With over 300 container routes linking more than 600 ports in over 200 countries and regions, the port has held the top spot in global cargo throughput for 15 consecutive years, and its container throughput has ranked third globally for six years in a row[④]. This highlights a maritime shipping and trade network that firmly establishes the port's connection to the world.

现代化深水大港。宁波舟山港由19个港区组成，面朝太平洋主航道，背靠中国大陆长三角经济圈，是中国大陆大型和特大型深水泊位最多的港口，也是全球唯一拥有双“千万箱级”单体集装箱码头的港口。

A Modern Deep-water Port. Ningbo Zhoushan Port, a comprehensive and strategic port comprised of 19 port areas, stands as a vital link to the busiest trade routes in the Pacific Ocean. Situated in the dynamic Yangtze River Delta economic region, it enjoys a well-connected hinterland. With the distinction of operating numerous large and super-large deep-water berths in Chinese mainland, it boasts the impressive accolade of being the world's sole port equipped with dual 10-million-TEU terminals. Such stellar infrastructure positions Ningbo Zhoushan Port at the forefront of global maritime trade.

全货种接卸能力。宁波舟山港是中国的主枢纽港之一，主要经营进口铁矿砂、内外贸集装箱、原油成品油、液体化工产品、煤炭以及其他散杂货装卸、储存和中转业务，是中国沿海向欧洲、美洲、大洋洲等地港口远洋运输辐射的理想集散地。

Capacity for Handling All Types of Goods. Ningbo Zhoushan Port, a prominent hub port in China, plays a pivotal role in handling (including storing and transshipping) a diverse range of cargoes, including imported iron ore, domestic and foreign trade containers, crude oil and refined oil products, liquid chemical

④ 资料来源：宁波舟山港股份有限公司官网。
Source: Official website of Ningbo-Zhoushan Port Company Limited.

products, coal, and other bulk commodities. With its strategic location, the port serves as an ideal distribution center for long-distance transportation, connecting China's coastal areas to ports in Europe, the Americas, Oceania, and beyond.

全配套服务保障。宁波舟山港现代物流服务综合实力持续提升，是全球少数拥有“船到船”LNG（液化天然气）同步加注服务能力的港口。2023 年，“宁波舟山”在新华·波罗的海国际航运中心发展指数排名升至第 9 位⑤。

Comprehensive Logistics Support. Ningbo Zhoushan Port has consistently enhanced its comprehensive strength in modern logistics services, positioning itself as a leading global port. Notably, it possesses the distinctive capability of providing "ship-to-ship" LNG (liquefied natural gas) synchronous refueling services, a rarity among ports worldwide. The port has achieved an impressive rise to the 9th position in the highly regarded 2023 Xinhua-Baltic International Shipping Center Development Index⑤.

（二）开放平台
Open Platforms

宁波以敢为人先的魄力逐浪前行，服务国家开放大局。

With a pioneering spirit, Ningbo forges ahead and contributes to the country's broader agenda of openness.

改革开放后，宁波依托保税区、出口加工区、保税港区、综合保税区、经济技术开发区等高能级开放平台走向国际化。

Since the reform and opening up, the city leverages high-level open platforms – such as bonded zones, export processing zones, bonded port zones, comprehensive bonded zones, and economic and technological development zones – to expand its international presence.

⑤ 资料来源：新华社中经社、英国波罗的海交易所，《新华·波罗的海国际航运中心发展指数报告（2023）》。

Source: Xinhua CEIS, UK Baltic Exchange, *Xinhua-Baltic International Shipping Center Development Index Report* (2023).

进入新发展阶段，宁波以中国（浙江）自贸试验区宁波片区和中国－中东欧国家经贸合作示范区“两区”建设，推动更深层次对外开放，为中国开放大局贡献“宁波力量”。

Ningbo is propelling itself into a new phase of development with the establishment of the Ningbo Area of China (Zhejiang) Free Trade Zone and the China-CEEC Business Cooperation Demonstration Zone. These initiatives bolster its international openness and play a pivotal role in strengthening China's overall openness. Known for its "Ningbo strength," the city is making valuable contributions to regional and global economic cooperation and integration.

中国（浙江）自贸试验区宁波片区。宁波围绕国际航运和物流枢纽、国际油气资源配置中心、国际供应链创新中心、全球新材料科创中心和全球智能制造高质量发展示范区“一枢纽、三中心、一示范区”功能定位，打造新

中国（浙江）自贸试验区宁波片区
Ningbo Area of China (Zhejiang) Free Trade Zone

时代对外开放的新高地。截至2023年，宁波片区已与200多个国家和地区建立贸易关系，累计引进外资项目2300余个，40多家世界500强企业落地投资⑥。

Ningbo Area of China (Zhejiang) Free Trade Zone. Ningbo prudently nurtures its core competencies as an international shipping and logistics hub, an international oil and gas resource allocation center, an international supply chain innovation center, a global innovation center for new materials science and technology, and a high-quality development demonstration zone for global intelligent manufacturing. Collectively known as "One Hub, Three Centers, One Demonstration Zone," these strategic pillars drive Ningbo to become a prominent frontier of openness and innovation in the new era, solidifying its position as a leader in regional and global economic development. As of 2023, the Ningbo Area has established robust trade partnerships with over 200 countries and regions, fostering a thriving global network. The region has attracted over 2300 foreign investment projects, with significant contributions from prestigious Fortune Global 500 companies⑥.

中国－中东欧国家经贸合作示范区。宁波拥有中国－中东欧国家博览会、中国－中东欧国家合作论坛、中国－中东欧国家市长论坛等品牌活动，建有中东欧工业园（中捷产业园）、中东欧贸易物流园、中东欧青年创业创新中心等平台，获批中国唯一的中东欧农食产品先行先试口岸，中东欧国家特色商品常年馆成为全国规模最大、品种最多的中东欧商品集散中心。宁波率先在全国实现中东欧国家"友城全覆盖"，设立索非亚中国文化中心，组建"一带一路"产教协同联盟。

China-CEEC Business Cooperation Demonstration Zone. Ningbo holds prominent events such as the China-CEEC Expo, CEEC Cooperation Forum, and CEEC Mayors Forum. It has established key platforms including the Central and Eastern European Industrial Park (China-Czech Industrial Park), the Central and Eastern European Trade and Logistics Park, and the Central and Eastern

⑥ 资料来源：宁波市商务局。
Source: Ningbo Municipal Bureau of Commerce.

中国－中东欧国家经贸合作示范区
China-CEEC Business Cooperation Demonstration Zone

European Youth Innovation Center. Moreover, the city has secured exclusive recognition as China's only pilot port for the trial import of agricultural and food products from Central and Eastern Europe. Additionally, the city's Central and Eastern European Commodity Perennial Pavilion stands as the country's largest and most diverse distribution center for Central and Eastern European goods. Ningbo has taken the lead in establishing friendly relations with CEEC cities, meanwhile setting up the Sofia China Cultural Center and launching the "Belt and Road" Alliance for Industry and Education Collaboration (BRAIEC).

（三）接轨国际
Going International

开放是宁波最大的优势，港口是宁波最大的资源。

The openness serves as the key advantage and the port as the greatest resource of Ningbo.

从2000年的“农民包机”奔赴广交会，到2022年的“涉外包机”开拓市场，宁波人始终在“甬动全球”的路上前行，也造就了宁波外贸硬实力。

The people of Ningbo have consistently advanced on the journey towards global participation, shaping Ningbo's robust foreign trade capabilities. For example, the city arranged chartered flights for farmer entrepreneurs heading to the Canton Fair in 2000 and for local entrepreneurs to explore foreign markets in 2022.

以商会友，宁波的国际“朋友圈”已拓展到世界54个国家的110个城市[⑦]，奏响与世界携手前行的时代乐章。

Ningbo has solidified its global presence and established cooperative relationships with 110 cities spanning 54 countries[⑦], creating a seamless network of collaboration and mutual benefit.

经贸联动。对外贸易是宁波的一张名片。如今，宁波深化推进“优进优出”强外贸、“双招双引”促外资、“组团出海”张藤蔓，2023年进出口总额1.28万亿元，晋升为中国外贸综合竞争力第四城，向内落地一批世界500强企业项目，对外加快布局“一带一路”沿线重要资源、技术和渠道，开放型经济发展始终走在全国前列。

Economic and Trade Cooperation. Foreign trade is a hallmark of Ningbo. Today, Ningbo optimizes imports and exports to strengthen foreign trade, actively attracts investment, talent, and foreign capital, and expands overseas markets through coordinated efforts. In 2023, its import and export volume reached 12.8 trillion yuan, elevating the city to the fourth most competitive in China's foreign trade. A batch of projects initiated by Fortune Global 500 enterprises

⑦ 资料来源：宁波国际友城40周年主题展开幕 [N]. 宁波日报，2023-5-25。
Source: 40th Anniversary Exhibition of Ningbo's International Friendship Cities Opens. *Ningbo Daily*, May 25, 2023.

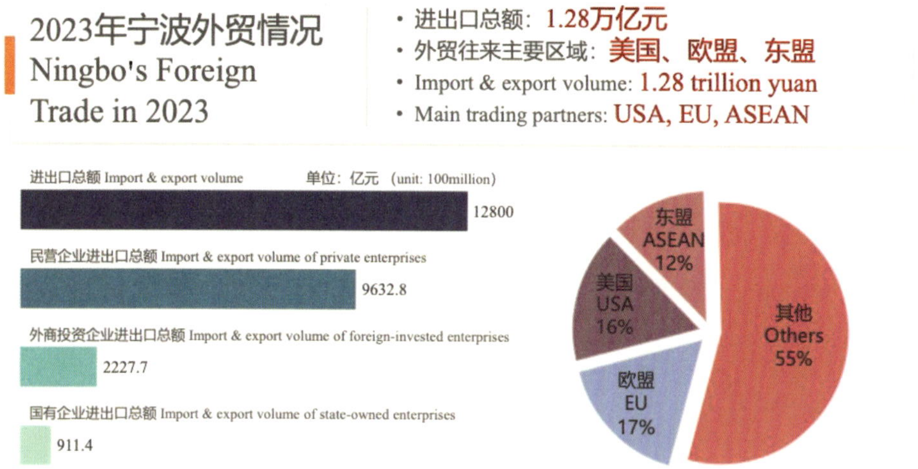

2023 年宁波外贸情况图　Ningbo's Foreign Trade in 2023

were established, while its international expansion was accelerated to secure key resources, technologies, and channels along the "Belt and Road". Its development of an open economy has consistently been at the forefront in China.

人文互动。1983 年，宁波与日本长冈京市结为首个国际友好城市。40 年来，宁波与全球其他城市的友好关系不断拓展，并为人员往来提供便利，进行公务商务包机申报流程优化，推行外商注册企业、工作许可、居留许可等“一件事”联审联办，实施外国人 144 小时过境免签。

People-to-people Exchange. Ningbo established its first international sister-city relationship with Nagaokakyo (Japan) in 1983. Over the past 40 years, the city continues to expand its friendly relationships with other cities around the world, facilitating people-to-people exchanges. The city has streamlined procedures for the declaration of official business charter flights, implemented joint reviews for foreigner-related affairs such as business registration, work permits, and residence permits, and initiated a 144-hour transit visa-free policy for foreigners.

丈量产业版图
Industrial Layout

前湾新能源汽车产业园　Qianwan New Energy Vehicle Industrial Park

宁波产业优势鲜明。以都市农业、先进制造业、现代服务业为主体的现代化产业体系，相互支撑、相互促进，持续推动宁波社会经济迈向新的高度。

Ningbo boasts distinct industrial advantages. Its modern industrial system, centered around urban agriculture, advanced manufacturing, and modern services, provides mutual support and promotes continuous growth, propelling Ningbo's socio-economic development to new heights.

（一）都市农业
Urban Agriculture

宁波农业历史悠久、资源丰富。近年来，宁波坚持和深化新时代“千万工程”，以“优质高效、特色精品、绿色生态、美丽田园、产业融合、健康养生”为导向，扎实推进农业强市建设，加快打造乡村振兴市域样板，打造了一批彰显宁波特色的农业产业，走出了一条具有宁波特色的绿色都市农业发展之路。2023 年，全市全面建成国家现代农业示范区，第一产业实现增加值 383.8 亿元，农副产品进出口额 409.1 亿元，占全省的 1/3，农业经济、农业现代化水平均保持全省全国领先。

Ningbo has a rich history and abundant resources in agriculture. In recent years, the city has committed to and deepened its efforts in the "Ten Million Project" for the new era, focusing on high-quality efficiency, distinctive premium products, green ecology, beautiful countryside, industry integration, and healthy living. This approach has solidly advanced the construction of a strong agricultural city, accelerated the creation of a model area for rural revitalization, and developed a number of agricultural industries that highlight Ningbo's unique characteristics. This has led Ningbo down a path of green urban agricultural development. In 2023, Ningbo fully established itself as a national modern agricultural demonstration zone. The primary industry achieved a value added of 38.38 billion yuan, and the import and export of agricultural and sideline products reached 40.91 billion yuan, accounting for one-third of the total of Zhejiang province. Both the agricultural economy and the level of agricultural modernization in Ningbo remain leaders at the provincial and national levels.

绿色基础产业。2023年，宁波实现农林牧渔业总产值630.1亿元，连续多年保持全省第一。聚焦粮食、生猪、蔬菜、水产品等主要农产品，宁波谋划启动奉化、宁海两个战略性蔬菜保供基地，加快推进新建猪场产能释放，大力推进海洋捕捞规模化、组织化发展，深入实施水产健康养殖“五大行动”，农业规模经营率超过70%，农作物综合机械化率接近90%。

Green Primary Industries. In 2023, Ningbo achieved a total output value of agriculture, forestry, animal husbandry, and fisheries of 63.01 billion yuan, maintaining the first place in the province for consecutive years. With a strategic focus on key agricultural products, including grains, pigs, vegetables, and aquatic items, Ningbo has laid out plans to establish two strategic vegetable supply bases in Fenghua and Ninghai. Additionally, the city is set to accelerate the production capacity of new pig farms, vigorously enhance the scale and organization of marine fishing, and implement five major initiatives for healthy aquaculture. These efforts have led to an agricultural scale operation rate surpassing 70%, and the comprehensive mechanization rate of crop production is now approaching an impressive 90%.

特色优势产业。截至2023年，宁波累计创建全国一村一品示范村镇28个，数量位居全省第一，拥有省“土特产”百品榜产品21个，培育了红美人柑橘、甬优种业、象山大白鹅、岱衢族大黄鱼等一大批新的农业主导产业和产品。主导产业产值占比达到80%。

Specialty and Competitive Industries. By the end of 2023, Ningbo has established 28 national demonstration villages and towns for "one village, one product" campaign, ranking first in the province in terms of quantity; meanwhile, its 21 products had been ranked on the provincial "Local Specialty" list, cultivating a large number of new leading agricultural industries such as Xiangshan Tangerines (*Hongmeiren* in Chinese pinyin), Yongyou Seeds, Xiangshan Big White Goose, and Dai-qu stock of Large Yellow Croaker. The output value of those leading industries accounted for 80%.

现代种业。种业是宁波推动现代农业发展的战略性、基础性产业。2023年，全市种业年产值超过43亿元，主要农作物良种覆盖率在98%以上。宁海县成为全省唯一的全国级制种大县，6家企业（机构）入选国家种业阵型企业，占全省的40%。

Modern Seed Industry. The seed industry plays a strategic and fundamental role in advancing Ningbo's modern agricultural development. In 2023, the city's seed industry generated an annual output value exceeding 43 billion yuan, with the coverage rate of high-quality seeds for major crops surpassing 98%. Ninghai County became the only national-level seed production county in the province, with six enterprises (institutions) being selected as national key seed industry enterprises, accounting for 40% of the province's total.

宁波农业在自身发展的同时，依托国家级现代农业产业园、国家农业产业强镇等数十个产业平台，不断与第二、第三产业互促发展。在农业与工业融合方面，截至2023年，宁波累计培育国家级农业龙头企业11家、农民合作社示范社33家，省、市级农业龙头企业374家，拥有10亿元以上省级示范性农业全产业链12条，产值亿元以上农业龙头企业87家，加工产业涵盖农林牧渔业等各个领域。在农业与服务业融合方面，宁波围绕价值链提升、销售链延伸、农文旅同步、数字链深化，培育中国农业品牌目录4个、省农业品牌目录16个，举办首届宁波农业博览会，推动创建全国休闲农业重点县、中国重要农业文化遗产、中国美丽休闲乡村、全国休闲农业精品线路等金字招牌，建成省级数字农业工厂45个、省级未来农场4个。

The agriculture of Ningbo has also been promoting its own integration with the secondary and tertiary industries via dozens of industry platforms such as national-level modern agricultural industrial parks and national strong agricultural industrial towns. As for the integration of agriculture and industry, by the end of 2023, Ningbo had cultivated 11 national-level agricultural leading enterprises, 33 farmer cooperative demonstration societies, and 374 provincial and municipal-level agricultural leading enterprises. It has established 12 provincial-level exemplary agricultural full industrial chains with a value of over 1 billion yuan, and 87 agricultural leading enterprises with a value of over 100 million

慈溪现代农业产业园 Cixi Modern Agricultural Industrial Parks

yuan. The processing industry covers various fields such as agriculture, forestry, animal husbandry, and fisheries. Regarding the integration of agriculture and services, Ningbo focuses on enhancing the value chain, extending the sales chain, synchronizing agriculture with culture and tourism, and deepening digitalization. It has nurtured 4 entries in the Chinese Agricultural Brand Directory, 16 entries in the provincial agricultural brand directory, hosted the first Ningbo Agricultural Expo, promoted the creation of national key counties for leisure agriculture, important agricultural cultural heritage in China, beautiful leisure rural areas in China, and national boutique routes for leisure agriculture, and established 45 provincial-level digital agricultural factories and 4 provincial-level future farms.

（二）先进制造
Advanced Manufacturing

宁波是中国重要的先进制造业基地，拥有中国模具之都、中国文具之都等 9 个行业之都称号，已形成绿色石化、汽车、高端装备等 8 个千亿级产业，培育了一大批专注于细分行业、具备全国乃至全球冠军地位的企业，国家级制造业单项冠军数量稳居全国城市第一位。

Ningbo is a vital hub for advanced manufacturing in China, holding nine industrial titles such as "Capital of China Mould" and "Stationery Capital of China". It has cultivated a robust industrial landscape featuring green petrochemicals, automobiles, high-end equipment, and several other industries surpassing the hundred-billion-yuan mark. It has nurtured a great many enterprises, positioned as national and even global champions, with a focus on specialized trade industries. Remarkably, Ningbo tops the list of Chinese cities by securing the highest number of sector champions of manufacturing nationwide.

未来，宁波紧盯高端化、智能化、绿色化转型，聚力打造数字产业、绿色石化、高端装备等3个万亿级产业集群，新型功能材料、新能源、关键基础件、智能家电、时尚纺织服装、现代健康等6个千亿级产业集群，以及一批新兴产业和未来产业群，加快构建现代化产业体系。

Ningbo is committed to driving high-end, intelligent, and environmentally friendly transformation, with a strong focus on cultivating three trillion-yuan industrial clusters (i.e., digital industry, green petrochemicals, and high-end equipment). Additionally, it aims to develop six hundred-billion-yuan industrial clusters specializing in new functional materials, new energy, key basic components, intelligent home appliances, fashion textile and clothing, and modern healthcare. Utilizing this momentum, Ningbo will also prioritize the establishment of emerging and future industrial clusters, further expediting the construction of a modernized industrial system.

数字产业。2023年，宁波数字产业集群总产值达4456.3亿元。依托北仑芯港小镇、余姚智能光电产业园、江北高新产业社区、宁波软件园等主要园区，宁波聚焦发展集成电路、光学电子与传感、电子材料、软件与互联网等细分行业集群，拥有甬矽电子（宁波）股份有限公司、舜宇光学科技（集团）有限公司、宁波兴业盛泰集团有限公司、宁波港信息通信有限公司等重点企业。

甬矽电子集成电路　Integrated Circuits of Forehope Electronics

Digital Industries. In 2023, the total output value of this cluster reached 445.63 billion yuan. Thanks to major parks such as Beilun Xin'gang Silicon Harbor Town, Yuyao Intelligent Optoelectronics Industrial Park, Ningbo Jiangbei High-Tech Industrial Park of Optoelectronics, and Ningbo Software Park, Ningbo focuses on the development of segmented industries including integrated circuits, optoelectronics and sensors, electronic materials, software, and the internet. Key enterprises in this cluster include Forehope Electronic (Ningbo) Co., Ltd., Sunway Optoelectronics Technology (Group) Co., Ltd., Ningbo Xingye Shengtai Group Co., Ltd., and Ningbo Port Group Information Communication Co., Ltd.

绿色石化。宁波绿色石化产业集群是全国唯一的石化产业国家先进制造业集群，2023 年总产值达 4959.4 亿元，产业规模居全国七大石化产业基地之首。依托石化经济技术开发区、北仑绿色石化产业园等主要园区，宁波聚焦发展化工新材料重点细分行业，拥有万华化学（宁波）有限公司、浙江逸盛石化有限公司等重点企业。

Green Petrochemicals. It stands as the sole national advanced manufacturing cluster in the petrochemical industry throughout China. By 2023, the total output value of this cluster has reached 495.94 billion yuan, ranking as the largest among the seven major petrochemical industry bases nationwide. Relying on key areas such as the Petrochemical Economic and Technological Development Zone and the Beilun Green Petrochemical Industrial Park, Ningbo focuses on the development of segmented industries including new chemical materials. It includes prominent enterprises like Wanhua Chemical (Ningbo) Co., Ltd. and Zhejiang Yisheng Petrochemical Co., Ltd.

绿色石化园区 Green Petrochemical Industrial Park

高端装备。2023 年，宁波高端装备产业集群总产值达 7956.8 亿元。依托前湾新能源汽车产业园、北仑小港装备产业社区等主要园区，聚焦发展节能与新能源汽车、智能成型装备与机器人等重点细分行业，拥有吉利集团（宁波）有限公司、宁波海天精工股份有限公司等重点企业。

High-end Equipment. In 2023, the total output value of this cluster has reached 795.68 billion yuan. Leveraging major parks such as Qianwan New Energy Vehicle Industrial Park and Beilun Xiaogang Equipment Industrial Park, Ningbo focuses on the development of segmented industries including energy-saving and new energy vehicles, intelligent forming equipment, and robotics. Key enterprises include Geely Group (Ningbo) Co., Ltd. and Ningbo Haitian Precision Machinery Co., Ltd.

新型功能材料。宁波新型功能材料产业集群是首批国家级战略性新兴产业集群，2023 年总产值达 2364.7 亿元。依托奉化滨海新材料产业园、宁波江北先进功能材料产业平台、高新区新材料产业园等主要园区和平台，宁波聚焦发展稀土磁性材料、高端金属材料、功能膜材料等重点细分行业，拥有宁波复能稀土新材料股份有限公司、宁波金田铜业（集团）股份有限公司、宁波长阳科技股份有限公司等重点企业。

New Functional Materials. It is among the first batch of national-level strategic emerging industry clusters, with a total output value of 236.47 billion yuan by 2023. Relying on key areas such as Fenghua Coastal New Materials Industrial Park, Ningbo Jiangbei Advanced Functional Materials Industrial Platform, and High-tech Zone New Materials Industrial Park, Ningbo focuses on the development of segmented industries including rare earth magnetic materials, high-end metal materials and functional film materials. Key enterprises include Ningbo Fonne Rare Earth New Materials Co., Ltd., Ningbo Jintian Copper (Group) Co., Ltd., and Ningbo Solartron Technology Co., Ltd.

新能源。2023 年，宁波新能源产业集群总产值达 2003.4 亿元。依托南湾光伏储能产业园、望春工业园区新能源产业园等主要园区，宁波聚焦发展智能光伏、电池及储能等细分行业，拥有东方日升新能源股份有限公司、中银（宁波）

电池有限公司等重点企业。

New Energy. By 2023, the total output value of this cluster has reached 200.34 billion yuan. Leaning on major industrial parks such as the Nanwan Photovoltaic Energy Storage Industrial Park and New Engery Industrial Park of Wangchun Industrial Zone, Ningbo focuses on the development of sub-sectors like smart photovoltaics, batteries, and energy storage. The cluster includes leading enterprises such as Risen Energy Co., Ltd. and Zhongyin (Ningbo) Battery Co., Ltd.

吉利极氪 001 汽车 Geely ZEEKR 001

关键基础件。2023 年宁波关键基础件产业集群总产值达 1289.6 亿元，铸造模具、压铸模具、核电站密封件、高端海底电缆等产品全国市场占有率已超过 50%。依托灵峰现代产业园、奉化智能装备关键基础件产业园等主要园区，宁波聚焦发展高端模具、特种电机、气动件等重点细分行业，拥有浙江华朔科技股份有限公司、宁波杜亚机电技术有限公司、宁波亚德客自动化工业有限公司等重点企业。

Key Basic Components. In 2023, the total output value of this cluster has reached 128.96 billion yuan. Products such as casting molds, die-casting molds, nuclear power station sealing components, and high-end submarine cables currently hold a market share of over 50% nationwide.Relying on major industrial parks such as Lingfeng Modern Industrial Park and Fenghua Intelligent Equipment (Key Basic Components) Industrial Park, efforts have been made to push key sub-industries, including high-end molds, special motors, and pneumatic components. The region

boasts leading enterprises such as Zhejiang Huashuo Technology Co., Ltd., Ningbo Dooya Mechanic & Electronic Technology Co., Ltd., and AirTAC (China) Co., Ltd.

智能家电。宁波是全国家电四大生产和出口基地之一，2023年智能家电产业集群总产值达1458.6亿元。依托余慈智能小家电产业园、慈溪智能家居产业园等主要园区，宁波聚力推动家电与人工智能、物联网、云计算、大数据等新一代信息技术深度融合，聚焦发展智能厨电重点细分行业，拥有宁波方太厨具有限公司、奥克斯集团有限公司等重点企业。

Smart Home Appliances. Ningbo is one of China's four major production and export bases for home appliances. In 2023, the total output value of this cluster has reached 145.86 billion yuan. Drawing on the strengths of main industrial parks like the Yuyao Smart Small Home Appliance Industrial Park and the Cixi Smart Home Industry Park, Ningbo focuses on deeply integrating home appliances with cutting-edge information technologies, such as artificial intelligence, the Internet of Things, cloud computing, and big data; key segments within the smart kitchen appliance industry are high on its list of priorities. Key enterprises in this sector include Ningbo Fotile Kitchenware Co., Ltd. and Aux Group Co., Ltd.

锦浪科技光伏 Ginlong Solis

时尚纺织服装。2023 年，宁波时尚纺织服装产业集群总产值达 1274.4 亿元。作为“红帮裁缝”发源地，宁波拥有全国最大的色纺纱生产基地、提花织造基地以及涤纶短纤维、针织品和服装生产基地。依托海曙临空纺织服装产业园、象山爵溪产业社区等重点园区，宁波培育了上千家时尚纺织服装企业，塑造了雅戈尔、申洲国际等国际知名品牌。

Fashion Textiles and Clothing. In 2023, the total output value of this cluster has reached 127.44 billion yuan. As the birthplace of the renowned Hongbang tailors, Ningbo boasts the largest production base in the country for colored spun yarns, jacquard weaving, polyester staple fiber, knitwear and garments. Relying on key

industrial areas such as the airport-based textile and garment industry in Haishu and the Juexi Industrial Community in Xiangshan, the city has cultivated thousands of fashion textile and garment enterprises, and shaped internationally recognized brands like Youngor and Shenzhou International.

现代健康。2023年，宁波现代健康产业集群总产值达742.0亿元。依托宁波生物产业园（宁海）、前湾生命健康产业园、明州经开区智能医疗产业园等主要园区，宁波聚焦发展生物医药、医疗器械细分行业，拥有宁波荣安生物药业有限公司、宁波天益医疗器械股份有限公司等重点企业。

Modern Healthcare. In 2023, the total output value of this cluster has reached 74.2 billion yuan. Leaning on key industrial parks like the Ningbo Bio-industry Park (Ninghai), Qianwan Life and Health Industrial Park, and Mingzhou Economic and Technological Development Zone Smart Medical Industrial Park, the city has carved out developmental niches with distinct advantages in sub-sectors such as biomedicine and medical devices. Notable enterprises include Ningbo Rong'an Pharmaceutical Co., Ltd. and Ningbo Tianyi Medical Appliance Co., Ltd.

未来产业。面向长远发展，宁波将着力培塑前沿新材料、未来智能、元宇

雅戈尔服装车间　Youngor Workshop

宙、未来能源、空天科技、未来海洋、量子科技、原创新药及未来诊疗九大未来产业赛道新优势，持续提升产业基础高级化和产业链现代化水平，率先将宁波打造成为未来产业创新引领区、场景应用示范区、融合发展先行区。

Future Industries. With a focus on long-term development, Ningbo will strive to shape new advantages in nine future industry tracks, including cutting-edge new materials, future intelligence, metaverse, future energy, aerospace technology, future ocean, quantum technology, original pharmaceuticals, and future diagnosis and treatment. The city aims to continuously enhance the sophistication of industrial foundations and the modernization of the industrial chain. It strives to take the lead in establishing Ningbo as an innovative hub for future industries, a demonstration area for scenario applications, and a pioneering region for integrated development.

（三）现代服务
Modern Services

随着制造业发展水平持续提升，宁波的服务业得以快速发展，基本形成了以现代贸易、现代物流、现代金融等5万亿级产业和文化创意、旅游休闲、科技及软件信息、商务服务等5000亿级产业为支撑的现代服务业产业体系。2023年，宁波服务业增加值8528.5亿元，对宁波GDP增长的贡献率为50.6%，占宁波GDP的比重为51.9%，13家企业登上中国服务业500强榜单。

As the level of manufacturing development continues to rise, Ningbo's service sector has also experienced rapid growth, ultimately establishing a modern service industry system supported by five-trillion-yuan and five-hundred-billion-yuan industries. Among the former batch are mainly modern trade, logistics, and finance, and among the latter cultural creativity, tourism and leisure, technology and software information, and business services. In 2023, the added value of service sector has reached 852.85 billion yuan, contributing 50.6% to the GDP growth of Ningbo and accounting for 51.9% of the city's GDP. And thirteen companies from Ningbo were listed among China's top 500 service providers.

现代贸易。2020年以来，宁波口岸进出口总额始终保持在2万亿元以上，排在中国各口岸前列，拥有中基宁波集团股份有限公司、宁波世贸通国际贸易有限公司等一批重点企业。除传统货物贸易优势以外，宁波的新型离岸国际贸易、新型易货贸易和跨境电子商务等国际贸易新业态不断发展壮大，2023年全市服务贸易进出口总额1728.3亿元，居浙江省第二位。

Modern Trade. Since 2020, the total import and export volume through its ports has consistently exceeded two trillion yuan, ranking among the top in China. The city is home to major enterprises such as China-Base Ningbo Group Co., Ltd. and Ningbo Shimaotong International Co., Ltd. Beyond traditional goods trade, Ningbo has seen continuous growth and expansion in new international trade forms, including new types of offshore trading, counter-trade, and cross-border e-commerce. In 2023, the city's total service trade import & export volume reached 172.83 billion yuan, ranking second in Zhejiang Province.

现代物流。宁波现代物流产业基本形成了港航物流、区域分拨和市域配送三大服务体系，拥有浙江中外运有限公司等近300家A级物流企业。依托宁波（镇海）大宗货物海铁联运物流枢纽港、宁波经济技术开发区现代物流园区等综合性物流园区以及宁波国际航运服务中心等物流服务综合体，宁波供应链物流、大宗商品物流、冷链物流、保税物流等高端物流实现创新发展。2023年，宁波被纳入国家现代流通战略支点城市。

Modern Logistics. Modern logistics of Ningbo has essentially established three major service systems: port and maritime logistics, regional distribution, and urban delivery. The city boasts nearly 300 A-grade logistics companies, including Zhejiang Sinotrans Co., Ltd. With comprehensive logistics parks like the Ningbo (Zhenhai) Bulk Goods Sea-Rail Intermodal Logistics Hub Port and Ningbo Economic and Technological Development Zone Modern Logistics Park, as well as the Ningbo International Shipping Service Center and other integrated logistics service complexes, Ningbo has achieved innovative development in high-end logistics sub-sectors such as supply chain logistics, bulk commodity logistics, cold chain logistics, and bonded logistics. In 2023, Ningbo was included as a strategic pivot city in the national modern circulation strategy.

现代金融。截至2023年，宁波金融业总资产突破6万亿元，本外币存贷款合计余额突破7万亿元，拥有国家保险创新综合试验区和普惠金融改革试验区两大国字号金融改革招牌，宁波银行、通商银行、甬兴证券、东海航运保险等总部金融机构，以及保险科技产业园、中国保险博物馆、全国数字健康保险交易平台、武汉大学宁波国家保险发展研究院等保险功能型、创新型平台。

Modern Finance. As of 2023, Ningbo's financial industry has surpassed a total asset value of six trillion yuan, and the combined balance of local and foreign currency deposits and loans has exceeded seven trillion yuan. Possessing two nationally recognized financial reform symbols—the National Insurance Innovation Comprehensive Pilot Zone and the Inclusive Finance Reform Pilot Zone—Ningbo is home to headquarters of financial institutions such as Bank of Ningbo, Ningbo Commerce Bank, Yongxing Securities, and East Sea Marine Insurance. Additionally, the city features functional and innovative platforms like the Insurance Technology Industrial Park, China Insurance Museum, National Digital Health Insurance Trading Platform, and the Wuhan University Ningbo National Insurance Research Institute.

文化创意。宁波文化创意产业已形成以“影视宁波”“书香宁波”“创意宁波”“音乐宁波”为核心的产业体系，拥有宁波音乐港、宁波广告产业园、和丰创意广场、民和惠风和畅文化产业园等近百家市级文创产业园区和市级培育园区。2023 年，宁波获批首批国家文化与金融合作示范区。

Cultural Creativity. The industry has formed a system centralized around key city brands in relation to film & TV, book-reading, creativity, and music. The city is host to nearly a hundred municipal-level cultural and creative industrial parks and cultivation zones, including Ningbo Music Port, Ningbo Advertising Industrial Park, Hefeng Creative Square, and Minhe Huifenghechang Cultural Industrial Park. In 2023, Ningbo was approved as one of the first national demo zones for cultural and financial cooperation.

旅游休闲。宁波旅游休闲产业构建了以山海休闲游、邮轮游艇旅游、乡村旅游为主体的产业体系。近年来，宁波持续推动旅游与农业、工业、文化、养老、健康、体育等产业融合，打造了一批新兴旅游业态。

Tourism and Leisure. The city has built an industry system focused on mountain and sea leisure travel, cruise and yacht tourism, as well as rural tourism. In recent years, Ningbo has continually promoted the integration of tourism with other industries such as agriculture, industry, culture, elderly care, health, and sports, creating a range of emerging tourism formats.

科技及软件信息。宁波科技及软件信息产业以高新区、甬江科创区为核心集聚区，拥有宁波市软件园、宁波鲲鹏生态产业园、宁波工业互联网产业园等主要平台载体，呈现研究开发、创业孵化、技术转移、工业设计、知识产权等科技服务以及工业软件、工业互联网平台、嵌入式软件等软件产业齐头并进的发展格局。

Technology and Software Information. With the High-tech Zone and the Yongjiang Scientific Innovation Zone as core gathering areas, the industry is supported by major platforms such as Ningbo Software Park, Ningbo Kunpeng Ecological Industrial Park, and Ningbo Industrial Internet Industrial Park. The sector presents a coalescent development pattern that includes technology services like research and development, entrepreneurship incubation, technology transfer, industrial design, and intellectual property, as well as software industries encompassing industrial software, industrial internet platforms, and embedded software.

商务服务。宁波商务服务产业覆盖人力资源、会议展览、广告、专业咨询、会计、税务、法务、资产评估、勘察设计、节能环保等领域。尤其是在人力资源领域，中国宁波人力资源服务产业园先后获批成为国家级人力资源产业园、国家级人力资源服务出口基地，56家机构入围“2022年度浙江省人力资源服务机构综合100强”，数量居浙江省首位。

Business Services. This industry encompasses various fields such as human resources, conference and exhibition services, advertising, professional consulting, accounting, taxation, legal services, asset appraisal, survey and design, as well as energy conservation and environmental protection. Notably, in the field of human resources, the China Ningbo Human Resources Service Industry Park has been consecutively recognized as a national-level human resource industry park and a national base for the export of human resource services. A total of 56 organizations have been selected as the top 100 integrated human resources service agencies in Zhejiang province in 2022, the highest number among all cities in the province.

面向未来，宁波进一步迭代升级服务业发展体系，聚焦智造服务、港航服务、新型贸易、文化服务、高品质生活等5大领域，实施创新赋能、数智赋能、融合赋能、低碳赋能、变革赋能等5大行动，力争将服务业增加值占比提高到60%。

Ningbo will further upgrade its service industry development system, focusing on five major areas: intelligent manufacturing services, port and maritime services, new types of trade, cultural services, and high-quality living. The city will implement five major empowerment strategies, including innovation empowerment, digital and intelligent empowerment, integration empowerment, low-carbon empowerment, and change enablement, with the aim of increasing the proportion of the service industry's added value to 60%.

致敬先贤名家
Local Personages

月湖　Moon Lake

虞世南　Yu Shinan

王安石　Wang Anshi

王应麟　Wang Yinglin

王阳明　Wang Yangming

范钦　Fan Qin

朱舜水　Zhu Shunshui

黄宗羲　Huang Zongxi

王宽诚　K.C. Wong

童第周　T.C. Tung

贝时璋　Shitsan Pai

谈家桢　C.C. Tan

周信芳　Zhou Xinfang

陈逸飞　Chen Yifei

余秋雨　Yu Qiuyu

一方水土养一方人，宁波人杰地灵，古往今来，在工商科教文卫体等领域都涌现出了大量杰出的人才。生于斯，长于斯，宁波儿女从国内日益走近世界舞台中央，并在各行各业取得辉煌成就。

Ningbo takes pride in its abundance of exceptional talents across various fields including industry, commerce, science, education, culture, health, and sports. Its people are increasingly gaining recognition both domestically and internationally, making remarkable contributions and achieving extraordinary accomplishments.

（一）古代名士
Ancient Great Minds

宁波作为国家历史文化名城，涌现出了王阳明、黄宗羲等一批影响深远的大家，以及王安石等与宁波颇有渊源的文豪。他们在宁波著书立说、传道授业、传承薪火。他们笃学躬行、开拓创新、实事求是、经世致用，铸就了宁波城市文化精神的底色。沧海桑田，斯人已去，精神永在，遗泽犹存，千余年来对中国乃至世界产生了深远的影响。

As a national historical and cultural city, Ningbo has raised a number of influential cultural thinkers such as Wang Yangming and Huang Zongxi; also, the city bears close connections with notable literati politicians and other historic figures, like Wang Anshi. They wrote books, spread teachings, passed on knowledge, and ensured the continuity of their scholarly traditions in Ningbo. Through their diligent pursuit of knowledge and unwavering dedication to both theory and practicality, these remarkable individuals have shaped the very essence of Ningbo's urban cultural spirit. Their endeavors have not only fostered a deep appreciation for learning and innovation but also instilled a profound respect for the practical application of knowledge in real-life situations. Their legacy continues to inspire generations, forming an integral part of Ningbo's rich cultural tapestry. As time passes, their spirits remain eternal, leaving behind an enduring legacy that has profoundly influenced not only China but also the world at large.

虞世南。南北朝至隋唐时期的书法家、文学家、政治家。他直言敢谏，对当时的“贞观之治”起着积极的作用。他与欧阳询、褚遂良、薛稷合称唐初四大书法家，拥有正书碑刻《孔子庙堂碑》等代表作。他还编写了中国第一部完整的类书《北堂书钞》，共一百六十卷，为保存古代文化典籍作出了重要贡献。

Yu Shinan was a versatile figure during the Southern and Northern Dynasties, as well as the Sui and Tang Dynasties. As a talented calligrapher, literary scholar, and statesman, he fearlessly expressed his opinions and provided valuable advice, making instrumental contributions in shaping the famous "Zhenguan Era" and leaving a significant impact on that period of history. He and the other three prominent figures (i.e., Ouyang Xun, Chu Suiliang, and Xue Ji) were collectively known as the four great calligraphers of the early Tang Dynasty. One of his representative works in calligraphy is the engraved stele "Confucius Temple Tablet." He undertook the extraordinary feat of compiling Beitang Shuchao ("Extracts for Books"), the first comprehensive Chinese encyclopedia comprising an impressive one hundred and sixty volumes. This monumental work played a pivotal role in preserving and safeguarding ancient cultural classics for future generations to cherish.

王安石。北宋时期政治家、文学家、思想家、改革家，“唐宋八大家”之一。王安石担任浙江鄞县（今鄞州区）知县三年期间，清理县库存粮、救济灾民，兴修水利，尤其是疏浚东钱湖，使其重新成为造福民众的“万金湖”。王安石还在月湖边创办县学，推动形成了官学、书院、蒙学三个教学系统。千余年来，王安石在宁波的治政理念，一直福泽后世。

Wang Anshi was a statesman, literary figure, thinker, and reformist during the Northern Song Dynasty, known as one of the "Eight Great Prose Masters of the Tang and Song Dynasties". During his three-year term as the magistrate of Yin County in Zhejiang Province (currently Yinzhou District), Wang undertook initiatives to clear surplus grain from the county's storage, provided relief to disaster-stricken residents, and extensively improved water management. His notable efforts included the dredging of Dongqian Lake, transforming it into a "Lake of Great Value" beneficial to the local populace. Wang also established a county school by the Moon Lake, contributing to the formation of three educational systems: official schools, academies, and elementary schools. For more than a thousand years, his philosophy of governance in this land has been blessing future generations.

王应麟。南宋学者、教育家、政治家。著有《三字经》等传统文化经典。他慧眼识人，文天祥、陆秀夫等人经他选拔得中进士。他高风亮节，南宋灭亡后隐居乡里，闭门谢客，不向元朝称臣。他是宁波乃至中国文化史上的一座丰碑。

Wang Yinglin was an educator and politician in the Southern Song Dynasty. His creation, "The Three-Character Classic," stands as a miniature classic of traditional culture. Wang had a discerning eye for talent, and individuals like Wen Tianxiang and Lu Xiufu — two politicians and folk heroes — succeeded in the imperial examination under his guidance. Despite immense political pressure, he refused to submit to the Yuan Dynasty and instead chose to remain in seclusion, dedicating his life to scholarly pursuits and the study of ancient classics. His unwavering integrity and commitment to principles made him a symbol of righteousness and moral fortitude. He stands as a monument in the cultural history of Ningbo and even China.

王阳明。明代著名思想家、哲学家、文学家和军事家。精通儒家、佛家、道家，而且能够统军征战，是中国历史上立德、立功、立言“真三不朽”的圣人，被誉为明代第一流人物。创立阳明心学，提出的“心即理”“知行合一”“致良知”三大思想精髓，对中国乃至世界范围都产生巨大影响。

Wang Yangming was the most famous thinker, philosopher, writer and military man of the Ming Dynasty. Not only was he well-versed in Confucianism, Buddhism, and Taoism, but he also excelled in military strategy and warfare. A paragon of virtue, achievement, and wisdom, he is hailed as a truly immortal figure in Chinese history, earning the title of a preeminent figure of the Ming Dynasty. Wang Yangming established the "Yangming School of

Mind," with its core principles of "the mind is the principle," "knowledge and action are unified," and "cultivating the innate moral sense." These teachings have had a profound impact not only in China but also over the world.

范钦。明代嘉靖时进士，官至兵部右侍郎。一生爱书，在收集和保存文献方面贡献巨大。晚年在宁波创建了天一阁，聚书数万卷，为浙东藏书第一家，是中国现存最古老的藏书楼。

Fan Qin was an imperial scholar (*jinshi* in Chinese pinyin) during the Jiajing period of the Ming Dynasty, and served as the vice minister of the Ministry of War. Throughout his life, he had an insatiable love for books and made significant contributions to the collection and preservation of literature. In his later years, he established the Tianyi Pavilion (serving as his private library) in Ningbo, which remains as foremost collector in eastern Zhejiang and the oldest existing library in China housing tens of thousands of books.

朱舜水。明末学者、教育家，中日文化交流的先驱。他把中国的传统文化以及治国、生产、经济、建筑等方面的思想技术传播到日本，深深影响了明治维新。

Zhu Shunshui was a scholar and educator of the late Ming Dynasty, and a pioneer of cultural exchange between China and Japan. He played a crucial role in disseminating traditional Chinese culture and ideas relating to governance, farming, economy, and architecture to Japan. His profound influence on the Meiji Restoration of 1868 in Japan continues to be recognized and celebrated to this day.

黄宗羲。明末清初经学家、史学家、思想家、地理学家、天文历算家、教育家。他前半生抗清，名噪一时；后半生全身心投入著书立说、培养人才的事业。独创以“经世致用”为宗旨的学风，形成了中国学术史上占有重要地位的史学派别——浙东学派。

Huang Zongxi was a Renaissance man of the late Ming and early Qing dynasties, excelling in multiple fields including economics, history, philosophy, geography, astronomy, and education. In the first half of his life, Huang rose to prominence as a renowned advocate against the Qing Dynasty, fighting for the restoration of Ming rule. In the latter half, he dedicated himself wholeheartedly to scholarly pursuits, producing numerous influential works and actively nurturing talented individuals. His pioneering school of thought — "Application of Knowledge to Practical Matters" — formed the basis of the important historical academic tradition known as the "East Zhejiang School" in Chinese academic history.

（二）商帮巨贾
Merchants and Tycoons

从宁波到上海，从香港到台湾，再到海外，源于宁波的一批又一批工商巨子，把自己开拓创业的奋斗历程与家乡和民族的命运紧密地联系在了一起，造就了中国近现代史上辉煌的“宁波帮”传奇。

From Ningbo to Shanghai, Hong Kong to Taiwan, and beyond, the entrepreneurial spirit of successive generations of industrial and business leaders hailing from Ningbo has become intertwined with the destiny of their hometown and nation. Their unwavering dedication and remarkable achievements have played a pivotal role in the legendary success of the "Ningbo Native Merchants" in the modern history of China.

“邵逸夫星”“李达三星”“王宽诚星”“曹光彪星”……苍穹之上，有多颗以宁波人的名字命名的小行星。他们以强烈的创业精神和杰出的经营能力，成为推动中国经济发展的中坚力量，他们爱国爱乡，热心公益，造福桑梓，反哺社会，以独有的儒商气质和拳拳的赤子之心，在中国发展史上留下浓墨重彩的一笔。

In the vast expanse of blue sky, there are several asteroids named after individuals from Ningbo, such as the "Run Run Shaw Star", "Li Dak Sum Star", "K. C. Wong Star", and "Chao Kuang Piu Star". They have proven themselves to be true pioneers and trailblazers, steering the course of China's economic development with their unwavering commitment to innovation, integrity, and excellence.

Their remarkable achievements and enduring legacies serve as a testament to the indomitable spirit of Ningbo's entrepreneurial community.

继往开来，新甬商在全球经济舞台上纵横驰骋，雅戈尔、杉杉、方太等品牌蜚声海内外，“宁波帮”英才们不仅在世界舞台上演绎新的商业传奇，更把人生理想融入国家和民族复兴的伟大事业中。

Standing at the forefront of the global economic arena, Ningbo entrepreneurs are leaving an indelible mark in history. True industry leaders, their renowned brands such as Youngor, Shanshan, Fotile, and more, have garnered widespread recognition both domestically and internationally. Not only are they creating new business legacies, but they are also embodying their life's ideals through the noble pursuit of revitalizing our country and our nation.

严信厚。中国近代企业的开拓者，晚清实业家。他兴办了中国第一家机器轧花厂通久源机器轧花厂、浙江省第一家纱厂通久源纱厂、中国第一家银行通商银行和中国第一家保险公司华兴保险公司等。

Yan Xinhou was a trailblazer in the realm of modern Chinese enterprises and an industrious figure of the late Qing Dynasty. Yan established the Tongjiuyuan Machine Ginning Factory, China's first-ever mechanized cotton ginning facility, and also inaugurated the first yarn factory in Zhejiang Province. Moreover, he played an instrumental role in the establishment of Imperial Bank of China, the country's premier financial institution, as well as KCAL Insurance Agency, the pioneering insurance company in China.

朱葆三。近代上海工商界领袖、上海总商会会长。他兴办的实业领域涵盖五金、钢铁、航运、金融、纺织、水泥、造纸、榨油、保险等，他与叶澄衷、严信厚等人共同创办的中国通商银行是国内最早的华商银行。

Zhu Baosan was a prominent figure at the helm of Shanghai's business community during modern times, serving as the President of the Shanghai Chamber of Commerce. He set up industrial fields covering hardware, steel, shipping, finance, textile, cement, paper, oil, insurance and so on. Together with Ye Chengzhong, Yan Xinhou, and others, he co-founded the Imperial Bank of China, which became one of the earliest Chinese-owned banks.

包玉刚。公认的华人世界船王，中国造船业走向国际市场的开拓者。他一生爱国爱乡，为香港的稳定和回归、为中国的现代化建设、为家乡宁波的开发开放作出了特殊的贡献。

Yue-Kong Pao is widely recognized as the revered "Ship King" within the Chinese community, who earned his esteemed reputation through his remarkable achievements in the maritime industry. Throughout his life, he cherished his homeland, significantly contributing to the stability and reunification of Hong Kong, the modernization of China, and the development and opening up of his birthplace, Ningbo.

邵逸夫。电视电影制片人、慈善家。他积极投身于教育、科技、医疗等公益事业，资助大学、医院等基础设施建设。2002年，他创立了“邵逸夫奖”，奖励在数学科学、生命科学与医学、天文学方面卓有成就的科学家。

Run Run Shaw was a notable television and movie producer, as well as a philanthropist. He actively engaged in philanthropy, supporting education, technology, and healthcare by funding the construction of universities, hospitals and other infrastructure projects. In 2002, the prestigious Shaw Prize was instituted to recognize and honor scientists worldwide for their outstanding achievements in mathematics, life sciences, medicine, and astronomy.

王宽诚。香港中华总商会原会长，是支持国家建设和改革开放的香港工商界优秀代表。他出资创立了“王宽诚教育基金会”，支持国家选派留学生，培养高科技人才。

K.C. Wong, past President of the Chinese General Chamber of Commerce in Hong Kong, stands out as a remarkable figure within the Hong Kong business sector for his support of national progress. He founded the K.C. Wong Education Foundation, dedicated to promoting international student exchanges with China and developing high-tech expertise.

（三）科学巨匠
Scientific Giants

宁波素有尊重知识、崇尚创新、尊重人才的浓厚氛围。不仅有屠呦呦、顾方舟两位人民科学家，也拥有宁波籍两院院士122位（截至2023年），数量居全国第一[⑧]。

Ningbo is renowned for its profound culture of valuing knowledge, championing innovation, and honoring talent. The coastal city boasts an extraordinary academic environment, as evidenced by its distinguished residents, including the esteemed scientists Tu Youyou and Gu Fangzhou. Additionally, with the remarkable presence of 122 CAS and CAE academicians (as of 2023)[⑧], Ningbo emerges as a frontrunner in academia across China.

他们勇于创新，敢为天下先，鞠躬尽瘁，勇做科技浪潮的弄潮儿，为科学进步和全人类的福祉作出了巨大贡献，也始终心系家国，成就了宁波科学家精神的时代价值。

With a spirit of innovation and fearlessness, Ningbo scientists have made groundbreaking advancements, positioning themselves as pioneers on the global stage. Their dedication to ushering in waves of scientific and technological progress has not only contributed to the advancement of science but has also improved the well-being of humanity as a whole. Holding their nation close to heart, these scientists embody the essence of their times and continuously strive to fulfill the noble mission of scientific exploration and progress.

童第周。享誉海内外的卓越生物学家、教育家、实验胚胎学家，20世纪生物科学研究的杰出领导者，被誉为"中国克隆之父"，是中国科学院首批院士。

---

⑧ 资料来源：央广网，宁波籍院士增至122位 数量仍为全国第一。
Source: Number of Ningbo−native academicians has increased to 122, maintaining its top position in the country. CCTV. com.

T.C. Tung was a distinguished biologist, educator, and experimental embryologist, standing out as a prominent figure in the realm of biological sciences in the 20th century. Revered as the "Father of Chinese Cloning," he earned recognition as one of the inaugural CAS academicians.

贝时璋。中国生物物理学的奠基人，中国早期细胞学研究专家，致力于动物个体发育、细胞常数等研究，创立“细胞重建学说”，为中国生命科学事业作出了杰出贡献。

Shitsan Pai was a pioneering founder of Chinese biophysics. As an early Chinese expert in cytology, Pai dedicated himself to the exploration of animal development and cell constancy. He notably established the theory of cell reformation.

谈家桢。国际著名遗传学家，中国现代遗传学奠基人之一，在复旦大学建立了中国第一个遗传学专业、第一个遗传学研究所、第一个生命科学学院。

C.C. Tan was a internationally celebrated geneticist and a major founder of modern genetics in China. It was under his visionary leadership that Tan established the country's first genetics program, first genetics research institute, and first School of Life Sciences at Fudan University.

路甬祥。流体传动与控制专家，浙江大学原校长，中国科学院原院长，提出“系统流量检测力反馈”等原理，开发出系列新型电液控制器件与工程系统，推动电液控制技术取得重要进展。

Lu Yongxiang, a distinguished expert in fluid transmission and control, served as the former president of Zhejiang University and the former CAS president. He spearheaded the principle of "system flow detection and feedback" and the development of groundbreaking electro-hydraulic control devices and engineering systems, significantly advancing electro-hydraulic control technology.

屠呦呦。中国中医科学院首席科学家、诺贝尔生理学或医学奖得主、共和国勋章获得者，60 多年来致力于中医药研究实践，带领团队先驱性地发现青蒿素，是首位获得诺贝尔奖的中国本土科学家。

Tu Youyou, Chief Scientist of the Chinese Academy of Traditional Chinese Medicine, is highly esteemed as a Nobel Laureate in Physiology or Medicine and a recipient of the prestigious Order of the Republic. She has been dedicating over six decades to advancing Chinese medicine research, in which she led a pioneering research team in the discovery of artemisinin, a major breakthrough in the battle against malaria. Her noteworthy achievements earned her the distinction of being the first scientist of Chinese Mainland to receive a Nobel Prize.

（四）文艺名家
Prominent Literary Figures

近现代以来，宁波文艺界百花齐放，无论是笔墨丹青、传统戏曲，还是当代乐坛、妙手文章，在各领域都涌现出不少大师级人物。他们彰显了宁波城市的人文魅力，也架起了东西方文明沟通的桥梁，提升了世界文化艺术的多样性。

In modern times, Ningbo's literary and artistic circles have witnessed a vibrant renaissance, fostering numerous masters in various fields. From the captivating brushwork of ink painting and the mesmerizing performances of traditional opera to the soulful melodies of contemporary music and the profound prose of remarkable writings, a diverse tapestry of talent has flourished, enriching the cultural landscape of Ningbo and beyond. Their influence has infused the city of Ningbo with a rich humanistic charm, concurrently establishing a bridge of communication and understanding between Eastern and Western civilizations. In doing so, they contribute to the diversity of global culture and art.

周信芳。京剧表演艺术家，京剧“麒派”艺术创始人，为京剧艺术的传承和发展作出了重要贡献，与梅兰芳先生一道被誉为“梅芳麒韵”。

Zhou Xinfang was a celebrated Peking Opera actor, and in particular, founder of the "Qi" school — a unique vocal style. He played a significant role in elevating Peking opera to new heights. Zhou and Mei Lanfang are collectively recognized as greatest Peking Opera performers of the 20th century.

潘天寿。美术家、教育家，现代中国画教学的主要奠基人，擅长写意花鸟、山水，偶作人物，对诗词、篆刻、画论、画史等均有精深的研究。

Pan Tianshou, an accomplished fine artist and educator, enjoyed a distinguished reputation as a preeminent figure in the realm of modern Chinese painting pedagogy. Renowned for his expertise in depicting birds, flowers, landscapes, and occasionally figures, his artistic prowess extends beyond the canvas. He has made significant contributions to the fields of poetry, seal carving, painting theories, and the historical study of painting, leaving an indelible mark on the world of Chinese art.

沙孟海。当代书法大师，书法艺术驰名海内外，在史学、语言文字学、考古学、书学、印学等方面卓有建树，历任中国书法家协会副主席、西泠印社社长、浙江省博物馆名誉馆长。

Sha Menghai was a renowned contemporary calligraphy master whose art is celebrated both domestically and internationally. His exceptional achievements span various fields, including history, language and philology, archeology, epigraphy, and seal science. He had served as Vice Chairman of the Chinese Calligraphers Association, President of the Xiling Seal Engravers' Society (XSES), and Honorary Director of the Zhejiang Provincial Museum.

陈逸飞。著名画家、导演和文化实业家，专注于中国题材油画的研究与创作，在电影、服饰、艺术设计等诸多方面取得创造性成就。

Chen Yifei was a noted painter, director and cultural industrialist. With a specialized focus on researching and creating China-themed paintings, Chen had attained impressive achievements in such fields as film, fashion, and art design.

冯骥才。中国当代作家、画家、社会活动家，出版作品集近百种，被译成英、法、德、意、日、俄等十余种文字，画作有"现代文人画"之称。近年来，他热衷投身于城市历史文化保护事业。

Feng Jicai is a contemporary Chinese writer, painter and social activist. His works have been translated into over ten languages, including English, French, German, Italian, Japanese, and Russian. In addition, his paintings are praised as "modern literati paintings". In recent years, he has been passionately involved in the preservation of urban historical and cultural heritage.

余秋雨。中国当代作家、学者，以擅写历史文化散文著称，为中国了解世界、世界了解中国搭建新的桥梁，著有《行者无疆》《千年一叹》等。

Yu Qiuyu is a contemporary Chinese writer and scholar. He has gained a broad readership for his historical and cultural prose, building new bridges for the mutual understanding between China and other parts of the world. His representative works are *Travel No End* (2001) and *A Sigh in Millennium* (2002), etc.

（五）奥运冠军
Olympic Champions

海洋文明浸润下，宁波先天有着开拓进取、锲而不舍的人文精神。在奥林匹克的赛场上，宁波体育健将保持昂扬奋发的进取姿态，大放异彩。2022年9月，宁波被中国奥委会授予“奥运冠军之城”称号。

Thanks to its rich maritime civilization, Ningbo possesses an inherent spirit of exploration, perseverance, and humanism. At the Olympic Games, athletes from Ningbo have maintained a resolute and enterprising attitude, continually achieving remarkable performances. In September 2022, the city was awarded the commemorative "City of Olympic Champions" trophy.

石智勇。中国男子举重运动员，获得2016年里约奥运会举重男子69公斤级冠军和2020年东京奥运会举重男子73公斤级冠军。

Shi Zhiyong is a Chinese male weightlifter. He won the gold medal in the men's 69kg weightlifting final at the 2016 Rio Olympics and in the men's 73kg weightlifting final at the 2020 Tokyo Olympics.

汪顺。中国男子游泳运动员，获得2020年东京奥运会男子200米混合泳冠军。

Wang Shun is an athlete of the Chinese men's swimming team. He won the men's 200m individual medley at the 2020 Tokyo Olympics in July 2021.

杨倩。中国女子射击运动员，获得2020年东京奥运会射击女子10米气步枪冠军和10米气步枪混合团体冠军。

Yang Qian is a Chinese female shooter. She won two gold medals in the women's 10-meter air rifle competition and the 10-meter air rifle mixed team event at the 2020 Tokyo Olympics.

管晨辰。中国女子体操运动员，获得2020年东京奥运会体操女子平衡木冠军。

Guan Chenchen is a former Chinese women's gymnast. She won gold in the women's balance beam final at the 2020 Tokyo Olympics.

篇章二
Chapter Two

奔“甬”而来，凤凰筑巢
Hub of Brains and Start-ups

杭州湾跨海大桥 Hangzhou Bay Bridge

风来千帆竞，潮涌逐浪高。宁波瞄准建设世界重要人才中心和创新高地战略支点城市的目标，以海纳百川的姿态广开进贤之路、广聚天下英才，以城市之名致敬人才、成就人才。

With sails catching the winds, Ningbo surges forward towards a pivotal city in building a major global talent hub and innovation stronghold, embracing diverse talents from all over the world. A highly supportive platform is established to unleash their potential and achieve greatness in their respective fields.

在这里，来自五湖四海、为梦想而奋斗的你，可以拥有“更广阔”的创业舞台、感受“最贴心”的成长环境、创造“无极限”的成就荣光。

Here, individuals from all around the world are empowered to pursue their aspirations, thrive in a nurturing environment, and make boundless achievements.

群英汇集、奔“甬”而来，宁波也将因你而更精彩。

As talents gather and rush to Ningbo, the city becomes an even more vibrant and extraordinary place. Your presence will undoubtedly add to the brilliance and excitement of this dynamic city.

尽享人才服务
Talent Services

宁波东部新城 Ningbo Eastern New Town

宁波致力于构建全领域、全要素、全方位的人才服务网络，打响“宁波五优、人才无忧”服务品牌，营造“热带雨林式”的人才生态，在工作、生活、安居等各方面为海内外英才打造落地“第一站”。在宁波这块热土上，来自五湖四海的各类人才加速成长。目前，宁波全市人才总量约241万人，万名就业人员中R&D人员全时当量接近215人年，高技能人才占技能劳动者的比重约35%，科技创新领域三大科创高地高层次人才比例接近70%[①]。人才与宁波，正书写相互成就的新篇章。

Ningbo has been dedicated to building a comprehensive talent service network, which encompasses all sectors, factors, and aspects. The city is actively promoting its "Five Excellent Services" brand to create a flourishing talent ecosystem, akin to a vibrant tropical rainforest. This ecosystem provides an ideal "first stop" for outstanding talents from home and abroad in various aspects such as work, life, and housing. On this fertile ground in Ningbo, talents from all over the world are growing rapidly. At present, the talent pool in Ningbo totals around 2.41 million people. Among every 10000 employed individuals, there are nearly 215 R&D personnel each year. Highly skilled talents account for over 35% of the skilled workforce, and the proportion of high-level talents in the three major science and technology innovation zones is close to 70%[①]. Currently, talents and Ningbo are jointly crafting a new chapter of mutual success.

（一）无忧服务
Superb Services

围绕人才“引”“育”“用”“留”各个环节，宁波建立了覆盖更全面、指向更精准、支持更有力的“通则＋专项＋定制”人才政策体系，探索构建阶梯式人才自主培育体制机制。

Surrounding the entire cycle of attracting, nurturing, employing, and retaining professionals, Ningbo has established a more comprehensive, targeted, and robust talent policy system that combines general principles with specialized and customized policies. The city is exploring for a tiered system for the autonomous

① 资料来源：中共宁波市委人才工作领导小组办公室。
Source: Talent Office of CPC Ningbo Municipal Committee.

development of its talent base.

1. 通则政策：普惠性人才政策

General Principles: Inclusive talent policies.

政策优待：针对各层次人才，推出落户、继续教育、科技创新、便捷就医、绿色出行等多个方面的优惠政策。

Preferential Treatment: A range of preferential policies are rolled out targeting professionals at various levels, including easier processes for obtaining residency, continuing education, sci-tech innovation, convenient access to healthcare, and green transportation options.

创业优助：建立了“投”“贷”“融”“保”全链条人才企业金融支持体系。支持人才企业境内外上市，鼓励设立海外创新孵化中心、国际科技合作基地、国家引智基地、院士工作站、院士科技创新中心、博士工作站等各类平台。

Entrepreneurial Assistance: A comprehensive financial support system for talent-retaining enterprises, including investment, loans, financing, and insurance, has been established. Support is provided for talent-retaining enterprises to list domestically and internationally, and meanwhile, companies are encouraged to set up overseas innovation incubators, international science and technology cooperation bases, national centers for attracting intellectual talent, academician workstations, academician centers for sci-tech innovation, and post-doctoral research stations, among other platforms.

权益优护：鼓励实施“谁使用、谁评价”的人才评价机制，以“价值”“能力”“共享”为导向的人才使用机制以及更加灵活的创新激励机制，打造了“人才码”“甬上乐业”人力资源综合服务平台等场景应用，形成了行政、司法和社会共治的知识产权协同保护体系。

Enhanced Protection of Rights and Interests of Talents: Employers are encouraged to implement a talent evaluation mechanism oriented towards "value, capability, and sharing." This uses a flexible innovation incentive mechanism, and has led to the creation of human resources service Apps like "Talent Code" and the "Enjoy Work in Ningbo" (*Yong Shang Le Ye* in Chinese pinyin). This has resulted in a collaborative protection system for intellectual property involving administration, judicial, and social governance.

子女优学：依托基础教育资源丰富优势，建立健全分层分类人才子女入学协调解决机制，让人才子女好上学、上好学。在具体政策落实方面，综合考虑不同人才类别、子女户籍和房产所在地等因素，通过统筹协调妥善安排。

Privileged Schooling for Kids: Leveraging the abundant resources in basic education, a well-structured system has been established to coordinate and resolve the school admission process for children of talents, categorized by different levels. This ensures that their children have easy access to education and receive quality schooling. In terms of the specific policy implementation, various factors are taken into account, including the type of talent, the child's residency status, and the location of their housing. Proper arrangements are made through comprehensive coordination.

安居优享：“货币补贴”与“实物配置”并举，既有租房补贴、安家补助、购房补贴等支持，也有人才社区、保障性租赁住房等供给倾斜，让人才在宁波工作舒心、生活安心。

Customized Housing Policies: The approach of "monetary subsidies + physical allocation" is adopted, which includes support through rental subsidies, settling-in allowances, and home purchase subsidies. There is also a preferential provision of talent communities and affordable rental housing to ensure that talents feel comfortable working and secure living in Ningbo.

2. 专项政策

Specialized Policies

宁波面向顶尖人才、科技领军人才和创新团队、青年科技人才、海外人才、卓越工程师、医疗卫生人才、教育人才及其他各类人才等特定人才群体，推出专项政策。尤其针对海外人才，对来甬开展科研合作或就职就业提供津贴补助或人才政策倾斜。

Ningbo has launched specialized policies targeted at specific talent groups, including top-tier talents, leading talents in science and technology, innovative teams, emerging sci-tech talents, international experts, exceptional engineers, healthcare specialists, educational practitioners, and other diverse talent categories. Special attention is given to international talents, offering them comprehensive incentives such as financial allowances, subsidies, and favorable talent policies to support their participation in research collaborations, or as they assume professional roles and employment opportunities in Ningbo.

3. 定制政策
Customized Policies

甬江实验室。赋予实验室人才引进聘用、项目组织管理、经费使用等方面充分的自主权，并在住房保障、子女教育等方面给予特定优惠政策，保障实验室人才的生活需求。

Yongjiang Laboratory (Y-LAB): The laboratory is granted full autonomy in aspects such as talent recruitment, project organization and management, and fund utilization. Specific preferential policies are provided in areas like housing security and children's schooling to ensure that the laboratory's talent needs are met.

重点用人主体。针对在甬高校院所、产业技术研究院及制造业“大优强”、单项冠军、专精特新“小巨人”等重点企业及产业人才项目给予一定政策支持。

Key Employers: Policies are in place to support key institutions and enterprises in Ningbo, including universities, research institutes, industry technology research academies, and leading manufacturing companies, "industrial champions," and specialized "little giant" companies, particularly with regard to talent projects.

重点发展区块。为以世界一流标准打造甬江科创区以及宁波前湾新区、宁波经济技术开发区、宁波高新区等重点区块、重点产业，差异化推出一批支持政策。

Key Development Zones: A suite of strategically differentiated policy supports has been unveiled to elevate key sectors and districts to world-class excellence, encompassing the Yongjiang Science and Innovation Zone, as well as prominent regions such as the Ningbo Qianwan New Area, Ningbo Economic and Technological Development Zone, and Ningbo High-Tech Zone. These targeted initiatives are designed to catalyze growth and innovation in these pivotal zones.

"宁波人才"微信公众号

WeChat Official Account of "Ningbo Talent"

（二）专属活动
Recruitment Events

宁波以"宁波人才日"及"中国浙江·宁波人才科技周"为双主线，采用"线上线下＋市内市外"联动方式举办了一系列重大人才活动，搭建起人才与城市的对话平台。

Ningbo has established a dialogue platform between talents and the city by organizing a series of significant talent-focused events in both online and offline formats, as well as within and outside the city. These events center around two main initiatives: Ningbo Talent Day and Ningbo Talents, Science and Technology Week, Zhejiang China.

宁波人才日。为营造尊才爱才浓厚氛围，2019年起，宁波将每年"谷雨"设为宁波人才日，取"雨生百谷、生机勃发"之义，推出"与宁波·共成长"人才工作总体品牌，打造宁波人才的专属节日，增强各类人才对宁波的认同感、融入感、归属感。因为一年一度的"谷雨之约"，越来越多的人才踏春而来，选择宁波作为"梦开始的地方"，逐梦甬城，留下"最美记忆"。

Ningbo Talents Day. To create a strong atmosphere of respecting and cherishing talent, starting from 2019, Ningbo has designated "Guyu" (Grain Rain;

6th Chinese Solar Term, usually falling from April 19 to 21) as Ningbo Talents Day, symbolizing the flourishing development that arises from the nurturing rain. Under the overall brand of "Growing Together with Ningbo", this initiative aims to establish an exclusive festival for talents in Ningbo, enhancing their sense of identity, integration, and belonging to the city. Thanks to the annual Talents Day, an increasing number of talented individuals are drawn to this city during the spring season. They choose to make Ningbo their home to pursue their dreams, creating cherished memories that will forever be engraved in the city's history.

中国浙江 · 宁波人才科技周。以“广聚海内外人才智力，博纳高科技创新成果”为主题。人才科技周通过开幕式和开放洽谈揽才、产业对接引才、学术交流聚才、赛事活动选才等 5 大特色主体板块活动，累计吸引 30 多个国家和地区、国内 200 余所高校和科研机构参会，形成引人才、引智力、引技术、引项目、引机构、引理念的良好态势。

Ningbo Talents, Science and Technology Week, Zhejiang China. This recruitment initiative is centered around the theme of attracting talents, fostering high-tech innovations, and bringing together brilliant minds, domestic and international. This event draws talents from all corners of the globe, organizing high-tech innovations. With its diverse activities, including the opening ceremony, open negotiations, industry matching, academic exchanges, as well as selective talent events and activities, it has successfully attracted participants from over 30 countries and regions, as well as more than 200 domestic universities and research institutions. This has resulted in a fruitful environment for attracting talents, knowledge, technology, projects, institutions, and innovative concepts.

高层次人才智力引进洽谈会（简称“高洽会”）作为“中国浙江 · 宁波人才科技周”的主要活动之一，是宁波年度规模最大的招聘盛会。宁波围绕自身产业结构特点、城市发展需求，持续引进一批高学历、高层次人才。每年吸引 1000 余家企事业单位、全国 200 余所高校的万余名高学历人才前来

中国浙江·宁波人才科技周现场
Ningbo Talents, Science and Technology Week, Zhejiang China

对接[②]。

Ningbo High-Level Talents Recruitment Fair is not only a major event of Ningbo Talents, Science and Technology Week, Zhejiang China but also the largest annual recruitment event in Ningbo. It stands as a premier platform that aligns with the industrial structure and urban development needs of Ningbo. With a dedicated focus on attracting highly educated and talented individuals, the fair consistently brings forth a multitude of promising candidates who can contribute to the growth

② 资料来源：宁波市人力资源和社会保障局。
Source: Ningbo Municipal Human Resources and Social Security Bureau.

and progress of Ningbo. Over 800 enterprises and institutions have been drawn to this highly anticipated event every year. With its broad reach, the fair attracts nearly 10000 doctoral and master's degree students from more than 100 colleges and universities nationwide②.

其他活动。除了重点品牌活动，针对广大来甬人才的不同需求，宁波市推出了一揽子人才活动：面向高层次人才的研修培训活动，人才专场音乐会、新春游园会、跨年演讲、人才沙龙等形式丰富的联谊交流活动，针对人才及企业投融资的金融对接活动等。

Miscellaneous Events. In addition to key brand events, Ningbo has launched a comprehensive suite of activities catering to the diverse needs of talents coming to the city. These include advanced training programs for high-level talents, special concerts, Spring Festival garden parties, New Year speeches, talent salons, and a variety of networking events, as well as financial matchmaking activities for talent and enterprise investment and financing.

（三）集聚高地
Talent Highlands

大平台是各类创新资源的“蓄水池”，也是高端人才栖息的“梧桐树”。宁波依托甬江科创区“顶配型”发展平台和20个开发区（园区），持续点燃科技创新、产业进步与城市发展的星星之火，逐渐形成人才集聚的重要战略高地。

Grand platforms are "reservoirs" for retaining high-end talents and all kinds of innovative resources. With the Yongjiang Science and Technology Innovation Zone as a leading force and the support of 20 development zones and parks, Ningbo is dedicated to fostering scientific innovation, advancing industrial growth, and enhancing urban development. This thriving environment provides a fertile ground for entrepreneurial talents to flourish and realize their aspirations.

1. 甬江科创区。甬江科创区规划面积197平方公里，旨在打造立足宁波、服务区域、面向未来的世界一流科创策源中心。甬江科创区以科创主平台、人才新高地、都市未来城为主体，聚焦新材料、工业互联网、智能制造产业三大基础创新优势，重点谋划海洋经济、空天经济和生命健康三个未来发展方向。甬江科创区专项资金和甬江科创基金，正推动重大创新载体建设、重大科创平台招引和科创生态的培育。

1. Yongjiang Science and Technology Innovation Zone. The Yongjiang Science and Technology Innovation Zone, spanning 197 km^2, is poised to become a globally renowned center for scientific and technological innovation, serving Ningbo and the surrounding region as it embraces the challenges of the future. The zone serves as a vital platform for science and innovation, fostering talent and envisioning the city of the future. Prioritizing new materials, industrial Internet, and intelligent manufacturing industries, the zone also holds a steadfast focus on the development of the marine economy, aerospace economy, and life and health sectors. Furthermore, such initiatives as the Special Fund and the Innovation Fund are established to support the construction of significant innovation platforms, facilitate the introduction of major science and technology platforms, and foster the development of a dynamic ecosystem for science and technology innovation.

2. 开发区（园区）。包含3个市本级管理平台和17个区县（市）重点发展平台，其中3个市本级平台如下。

2. Development Zones (and Parks). Ningbo boasts three city-level management platforms and seventeen key district/county-level development platforms. The three city-level platforms are:

宁波前湾新区。宁波前湾新区拥有宁波杭州湾经济技术开发区、中意（宁波）生态园、宁波前湾综合保税区等国家级重点平台，是参与长三角区域一体化发展的标志性战略大平台。前湾新区加快引才汇智，打造“前程湾里”人才招引品牌，坚持项目引才和人才引资双向发力、全职引才和柔性引才交融并行、高端人才和青年才俊两头招引，构筑全市人才智力集聚高地。

甬江科创区效果图 Rendering of Yongjiang Science and Technology Innovation Zone

Ningbo Qianwan New Area. Ningbo Qianwan New Area serves as a significant strategic platform for promoting integrated regional development in the Yangtze River Delta. Equipped with national key platforms such as the Ningbo Hangzhou Bay Economic and Technological Development Zone, the China-Italy (Ningbo) Ecological Park, and the Ningbo Qianwan Comprehensive Bonded

Zone, it stands as a landmark destination for fostering economic growth and innovation. The Qianwan New Area is accelerating its efforts to attract and gather talents. It aims to create a talent attraction brand known as "Start up Your Career at Qianwan", focusing on a dual-strategy of bringing in talents through projects and attracting investments through talents. The area employs full-time recruitment and flexible talent attraction methods, targeting both high-end professionals and young, promising individuals, all in order to become a city-wide hub of talent and intelligence.

宁波经济技术开发区。由两个国家级开发区、三个国家级海关特殊监管区、一个中国（浙江）自贸试验区宁波片区深度融合而成，重点发展汽车、石化、装备制造等临港产业以及国际贸易物流、类金融等服务业。宁波经开区重视海内外引智工作，在项目培育、平台建设、优秀成果奖励等方面不断加大扶持力度，为海内外智力引进培育提供了强有力的政策保障。

Ningbo Economic and Technological Development Zone. Through the deep integration of two state-level development zones, three state-level special

宁波前湾新区　Ningbo Qianwan New Area

customs supervision zones, and the China (Zhejiang) Pilot Free Trade Zone, Ningbo has created a remarkable synergy. The city prioritizes the growth of port-based industries, including automotive, petrochemical, and equipment manufacturing. Additionally, it fosters the development of service sectors such as international trade, logistics, and finance, enhancing its global economic influence. The zone attaches great importance to attracting talent from both within China and abroad. By continuously increasing support in areas such as project development, platform construction, and rewarding outstanding achievements, it provides strong policy support for the introduction and cultivation of domestic and international talents.

宁波高新技术产业开发区。高新区大力发展新材料、生命健康、软件与信息技术等产业，持续引进建设高水平研发机构，集聚宁波市约1/3的重点研发机构、2/3的检测认证机构和1/2的公共技术服务平台、1/10的高新技术企业[③]，海内外院士、国家重点人才等高端人才密度居宁波市首位。近年来，高新区相继推出“高新精英计划”“高新精英资本引才计划”“高新精英软件人才引进计划”等高层次人才引进计划，体系化的人才培养机制不断释放人才创新动能。

Ningbo High-tech Industrial Development Zone. In recent years, the high-tech zone has greatly developed industries such as new materials, life and health, software and information technology, and continued to introduce and build high-level R&D institutions. Among the gathered entities are about 1/3 of key R&D institutions, 2/3 of testing and certification institutions, 1/2 of public technical service platforms, and 1/10 of high-tech enterprises across the city[③]. Its density

宁波经济技术开发区　Ningbo Economic and Technological Development Zone

③　资料来源：宁波高新区：奋力争先进位　打造一流园区 [J]. 宁波通讯，2023（13）：86-87.
Source: Ningbo High-tech Zone: Striving to Build a First-class Park. *Ningbo Newsreport*, 2023(13): 86-87.

宁波高新技术产业开发区　Ningbo High-tech Industrial Development Zone

of high-end talents such as academicians and national key talents ranks first in Ningbo. In recent years, the high-tech zone has launched a series of high-level talent attraction programs, including "High-Tech Elite Plan," "High-Tech Elite Capital-Talent Attraction Plan," and "High-Tech Elite Software-Talent Introduction Plan." These initiatives have established a systematic talent development mechanism that continuously unleashes new energy for innovation.

宁波高新技术产业开发区　Ningbo High-tech Industrial Development Zone

（四）支撑机构

Supporting Organizations

宁波人才发展集团有限公司。成立于2023年6月，深耕高端人才引聚、人才综合服务、人才科创投资、人才数字化运营、人才成长赋能等五大业务板块，聚力打造“全球高端人才引聚的市场化支撑平台”“全方位人才资本开发的专业化运营平台”“全生命周期人才服务的数字化创新平台”。集团下辖宁波东方人力资源服务有限公司、宁波经理学院、宁波人才服务有限公司、宁波人才培训有限公司、宁波东部科创产业发展有限公司等多家子企业。宁波人才发展集团充分发挥人才强国“生力军”、人才服务“排头兵”、引才聚

宁波人才发展集团有限公司 Ningbo Talent Development Group Co., Ltd.

才“新引擎”的功能作用，助力宁波建设世界重要人才中心和创新高地战略支点城市。

Ningbo Talent Development Group Co., Ltd. Founded in June 2023, the group is committed to excellence in the following five key business areas: high-end talent attraction, comprehensive talent services, investment in talent science and innovation, digital talent operations, and talent growth and empowerment. Through these strategic pillars, it aims to establish a market-driven support platform for attracting global high-end talent, a professional operational platform for holistic talent capital development, and a digital innovation platform for providing comprehensive life-cycle talent services. The group includes multiple subsidiary companies, such as Ningbo Oriental Human Resources Service Co., Ltd., Ningbo Executives Institute, Ningbo Talent Service Co., Ltd., Ningbo Talent Training Co., Ltd., and Ningbo Eastern Innovation and Industrial Development Co., Ltd. The group assumes a leading role in building a talent-strong nation, providing top-notch talent services, and acting as a driving force for talent attraction and aggregation. It actively contributes to Ningbo's strategic objective of positioning itself as a global hub for talent and innovation. By serving as a key catalyst, the group plays an instrumental role in accelerating the city's overall development.

“宁波人才发展集团”微信公众号
WeChat Official Account of the "Ningbo Talent Development Group"

寻找事业机遇
Career Opportunities

宁波东方理工大学　Eastern Institute of Technology, Ningbo

宁波始终坚持科技创新战略导向。从成立第一家专业科研机构、第一家厂办研究院，到引进重点产业技术研究院，聚焦产业创新，宁波科创平台由少变多、从弱到强。进入新时代，宁波瞄准建设高水平创新型城市的目标，深化打造国家自主创新示范区，大力实施科技创新“栽树工程”，作为吸引高层次人才的关键载体。

Ningbo has consistently committed itself to the strategic focus on scientific and technological innovation. Over the years, this coastal city's science and innovation platforms have evolved from being scarce and underdeveloped to plentiful and robust. This transformation is marked by the creation of specialized scientific research institutions, factory-based research centers, and key industrial technology research institutes dedicated to industrial innovation. The city is to become a top-tier innovative metropolis by actively setting up high-level innovation platforms. As the demand for talents increases, Ningbo is well-prepared to attract and cultivate them, among which the city has become the first prefecture-level city to participate in the National Natural Science Foundation's joint fund.

（一）科研实验
Labs

截至 2023 年，宁波拥有省部级以上实验室 47 家，A 类市级重点实验室 30 家④，3 家入选全省重点实验室。面向未来，宁波将高水平打造以甬江实验室为引领的新型实验室体系。

Ningbo has developed a comprehensive laboratory system with 47 laboratories at the provincial/ministerial level or above, 30 new A-class municipal key laboratories and 3 Zhejiang key laboratories as of 2023④. The construction of this laboratory system is to be forward-looking and high-level, revolving around Yongjiang Laboratory.

④ 资料来源：宁波市科学技术局。
Source: Ningbo Science and Technology Bureau.

甬江实验室（新材料浙江省实验室）。成立于2021年5月，是宁波历史上投资规模最大的科创“栽树工程”，是浙江省政府批准设立的专注于新材料及相关领域研究的具有独立事业单位法人资格的新型科研机构。实验室以建成特色鲜明的世界级研究机构为愿景，围绕全球科技前沿和地方产业高质量发展需求，已在电子信息材料与器件、绿色化工、新能源材料、功能性结构材料、前沿材料、智能制造与高端装备等领域形成“十大中心、五大平台”科研布局。截至2023年，甬江实验室累计引进16支科研团队，35位学术带头人均来自世界顶尖学府、国际一流研发机构和全球头部企业，总人数达到430人。

甬江实验室一期创园 InnoPark 效果图
Rendering of InnoPark, Yongjiang Laboratory Phase I

十大中心 Centers		
新型显示与感知研究中心 Advanced Display and Sensing Research Center	先进电驱系统研究中心 Advanced Electrical Machine Drive Research Center	精准光子集成研究中心 Precision Integrated Photonics Research Center
无机氧化硅材料可控制备研究中心 Controllable Preparation and Application of silica Research Center	智能控制与系统研究中心 Intelligent Control and Systems Research Center	碳纳米新能源材料研究中心 Nanocarbon New Energy Materials Research Center
热场材料创新中心 The Thermal Field Materials Innovation Center	3D数字制造创新中心 3D Manufacturing Innovation Center	功能材料与器件异构集成研究中心 Functional Materials and Devices Heterogeneous Integration Research Center
先进结构陶瓷研究中心 Advanced Structural Ceramics Research Center		

五大平台 Facilities		
材料分析与检测平台 Material Analytical and Test Center	信息材料与微纳器件制备平台 Micro and Nano Devices Fabrlcatilon Center	材料数字化研发平台 Material Digitalization Center
绿色化工新材料中试验证平台 Green Chemical Materials Development Center	工程化验证与成果转化平台 Engineering Verification and Walidation Center	

甬江实验室科学研究方向和领域
Scientific Research Directions and Fields of Yongjiang Laboratory

Yongjiang Laboratory (Y-LAB; Zhejiang Provincial Laboratory of New Materials) Established in May 2021, Y-LAB represented the largest investment in Ningbo's history of science and innovation (known as the "tree-planting project"). The laboratory, approved by the Zhejiang Provincial Government, is a new type of research institution with independent legal entity status specializing in new materials and related fields. Y-LAB aspires to become a distinctive world-class research institution, focusing on the cutting edge of global science and technology and the high-quality development of local industries. A research framework of "ten centers and five platforms" has been established in electronic information materials and devices, green chemical engineering, new energy materials, functional structural materials, advanced materials, as well as intelligent manufacturing and high-end equipment. By 2023, Y-LAB has brought together a total number of 430 personnel (including 16 research teams and 35 leading academics), all from top-tier universities, premier research and development institutions, and leading global companies.

（二）主要高校
Major Colleges and Universities

宁波具有一批办学优质、特色鲜明的本科高校和高职学校。截至 2023 年，共有全日制普通本科高校 8 所（含武警海警学院），宁波东方理工大学（暂名）在筹。其中，国家“双一流”建设高校 1 所，浙江省首批应用型本科建设试点示范建设高校 4 所。拥有全职院士 29 名，国家级一流本科专业建设点 60 个，省级一流本科专业建设点 93 个，16 个学科进入 ESI 全球前 1%⑤。主要本科高校如下。

Ningbo is home to a number of high-quality universities and higher vocational institutions, including eight full-time higher education institutions offering degree programs (including China Coast Guard Academy) and Eastern Institute of Technology, Ningbo (tentative) as of 2023. Among these universities, one has been selected to participate in the national "Double First-Class" initiative, four universities designated as pilot demonstration universities for applied undergraduate programs in Zhejiang Province. There are 29 esteemed full-time academicians, 60 national first-class major construction sites, 93 provincial first-class major construction sites, and 16 disciplines listed in the ESI (Essential Science Indicators) Top 1% of world institutions⑤. The major colleges and universities are listed below.

宁波大学。1986 年由世界船王包玉刚先生捐资创立。学校是国家“双一流”建设高校（力学学科为“双一流”建设学

⑤ 资料来源：宁波市教育局。
Source: Ningbo Education Bureau.

科）、浙江省高水平建设高校（水产学科为登峰学科）。拥有12个学科门类，有一级学科博士学位授权点9个，博士后科研流动站9个，一级学科硕士学位授权点31个，硕士专业学位授权类别27个，本科招生专业59个。12个学科进入ESI全球前1%。拥有全职院士11名（其中中国科学院院士、中国工程院院士5名），省部共建国家重点实验室1个。实现了国家自然科学奖、国

宁波大学　Ningbo University

家科技进步奖、国家技术发明奖三大奖项的全面突破。

Ningbo University. Ningbo University, founded in 1986 by Sir Yue-Kong Pao (the renowned founder of Hong Kong's Worldwide Shipping Group), is an esteemed institution that has been selected as part of the prestigious "Double First-Class" Initiative in China; mechanics is designated as its "Double First-Class" construction discipline. The university is also acknowledged as a high-level construction university in Zhejiang Province, with its aquaculture discipline highlighted as Peak Discipline. It boasts a comprehensive academic structure with 12 disciplines, offering 9 first-level doctoral programs, 9 post-doctoral research stations, 31 first-level master's programs, and 27 master's professional degree programs, alongside 59 undergraduate programs. Remarkably, 12 of its disciplines rank within ESI Global

宁波工程学院 Ningbo University of Technology

Top 1%. There are 11 full-time academicians, including 5 CAS and CAE members, and a national key laboratory jointly established by China Ministry of Science and Technology and Zhejiang Province. Its significant breakthroughs in all the three major national science and technology awards cover the State Preeminent Science and Technology Award, the State Scientific and Technological Progress Award, and the State Technological Invention Award.

学校官网（NBU Official Website）：https://www.nbu.edu.cn

宁波工程学院。浙江省、宁波市共建，以市为主的全日制普通本科院校，硕士学位授予单位。学院以工科为主，文、理、经、管多学科协调发展，国家首批“卓越工程师教育培养计划”实施高校、国家首批产教融合建设高校、

国家教育强国项目和全国首批现代产业学院立项建设高校。“材料科学”和“化学”两个学科进入ESI全球前1%。土木工程、计算机科学与技术、化学工程与工艺、机械设计制造及其自动化、物流管理5个专业入选国家级一流本科专业建设点。宁波工程学院为宁波的绿色石化、智能制造、数字经济等领域输送了大量人才。

Ningbo University of Technology (NBUT). NBUT, jointly built by Zhejiang provincial government and Ningbo Municipality but with city taking the lead, is authorized to award master's degrees. The university focuses on the disciplines of engineering, while promoting the coordinated development of disciplines in humanities, science, economics, and management. It is among the first batch of universities to implement the "Excellent Engineer Education Training Program", "National Industry-Education Integration Initiative", "National Initiative of Modernizing Education", and among the first group of universities to establish modern industry colleges. Two of its disciplines, Material Sciences and Chemistry, rank in ESI Global Top 1%. Five majors, including Civil Engineering, Computer Science and Technology, Chemical Engineering and Process, Mechanical Design Manufacturing and Automation, and Logistics Management, have been selected as national first-class major construction sites. The university has cultivated a large number of talents for the sectors of green petrochemical, intelligent manufacturing, and digital economy in Ningbo.

学校官网（NBUT Official Website）：https://www.nbut.edu.cn

浙大宁波理工学院。浙江省人民政府管理、宁波市人民政府举办、浙江大学支持办学的全日制公办普通本科高校。形成以工科为主，理、文、法、经、管等相互支撑、协调发展的学科专业体系。打造数字化设计与制造、智慧化港口与服务两大学科群，集聚相关学科联动发展，建成省重点学科6个、市重点学科19个，在建“十四五”省一流学科5个。该校现有各类联合研究机构30个，形成立足区域、面向全国，政、产、学、研相结合的社会服务体系。学院坚持以国际化办学为特色，已与20个国家（地区）50余所高校建立校际合作关系。

NingboTech University (NingboTech). NingboTech is a full-time public

浙大宁波理工学院　NingboTech University

university managed by Zhejiang Provincial People's Government, founded by Ningbo Municipal Government, and supported by Zhejiang University. The university has developed a comprehensive system of disciplines that primarily focuses on engineering, harmoniously developed alongside disciplines in science, humanities, law, economics, and management. After years of efforts in digital design and manufacturing as well as intelligent port services, NingboTech has established six provincial key disciplines and nineteen municipal key disciplines, with five more provincial-level leading disciplines under development during the 14th Five-Year Plan period (2021-2025). Currently equipped with 30 joint research institutes, the university has formed a locally-rooted but nationally-oriented social service system integrating governments, industries, universities and research institutes. Internationalization features its educational system, as can be seen in its partnerships forged with over 50 institutions across 20 countries and regions.

学校官网（NingboTech Official Website）：https://www.nbt.edu.cn

浙江万里学院。多学科协调发展的应用型大学，全国深化创新创业教育改革示范高校、浙江省应用型建设试点示范学校。拥有硕士学位点3个，国家级一流本科专业建设点11个，国家特色专业4个，省一流学科6个（A类1个），专业水平建设2年蝉联校友会浙江省应用型高校第一名。学校与30余个国家和港澳台地区的80余所院校建立了合作关系。

浙江万里学院　Zhejiang Wanli University

Zhejiang Wanli University (ZWU). ZWU, a multidisciplinary application-oriented university, is selected as a national model university in deepening the innovation and entrepreneurship education reform, and a provincial model pilot university in constructing applied universities. The university boasts 3 master's degree programs, 11 national first-class major construction sites, 4 national characteristic majors and 6 provincial first-class disciplines (including 1 A-category). Notably, the quality of its undergraduate programs has topped the CUAA rankings among applied universities in Zhejiang Province for the last two years. Its inter-university cooperation has also been established with more than 80 institutions in more than 30 countries and regions (including Hong Kong, Macao and Taiwan).

学校官网（ZWU Official Website）: https://www.zwu.edu.cn

宁波诺丁汉大学。中国第一所具有独立校园、独立法人资格的中外合作大学，由世界百强高校英国诺丁汉大学与浙江万里学院合作创办，于2004年批准筹建。学校引进英国诺丁汉大学质量保障体系，师资由英国诺丁汉大学选聘或按同等标准全球招聘，颁发与英国诺丁汉大学完全一致的学位证书。建校20年来，该校培养了2万余名本硕博学生，近九成毕业生进入世界一流名校、名企深造就业。学校的创建为加深中英两国交流合作发挥了积极作用。

宁波诺丁汉大学　University of Nottingham Ningbo China

University of Nottingham Ningbo China (UNNC). UNNC stands as the first Sino-foreign cooperative university in China to have its own campus and independent legal entity status. With the full approval of the Chinese Ministry of Education,it was jointly established in 2004 by the University of Nottingham, a top 100 global university from the UK, and Zhejiang Wanli University, a key player in the education sector in China. UNNC remains consistent with the UK campus of the University of Nottingham by adopting its quality assurance system and recruiting faculty members globally with the same standards of or directly appointed by the UK campus, so as to ensure the awarded degrees identical to those offered in the UK. Over the past two decades, more than 20000 students across undergraduate, master's and doctoral levels have graduated from the university. Remarkably, nearly 90% of the graduates have advanced to top-tier universities and companies worldwide for further studies or employment. The establishment of UNNC has played a significant role in deepening the exchange and cooperation between China and the UK.

学校官网（UNNC Official Website）：https://www.nottingham.edu.cn/

宁波财经学院。始建于 2001 年，是一所以经济、管理学科为主，多学科协调发展的地方应用型本科高校，主要培养财经商科类人才。现有国家级一流本科专业建设点 4 个，省级一流本科专业建设点 7 个，省级新兴特色专业 4 个、优势重点专业 7 个。与国（境）外 50 余所高校及机构建立长期稳定的校际交流与合作关系。

宁波财经学院 Ningbo University of Finance and Economics

Ningbo University of Finance and Economics (NBUFE). Established in 2001, NBUFE is a local applied undergraduate university that focuses primarily on economics and management disciplines while promoting the coordinated development of multiple disciplines. The university with its main objective to cultivate talents in finance and business currently owns four national first-class major construction sites, seven provincial first-class major construction sites, four provincial-level emerging characteristic majors, and seven provincial-level key majors. Its long-term stable exchange and cooperation relationships have been established with more than 50 institutions from foreign countries and regions (including Hong Kong, Macao and Taiwan).

学校官网（NBUFE Official Website）：https://www.nbufe.edu.cn

宁波大学科学技术学院。成立于1999年4月，是实施本科层次学历教育的全日制普通高等学校，全国先进独立学院。学院主动融入地方经济，走出了一条特色鲜明的产教融合和应用型转型新路径。获批省级重点支持现代产业学院2个、省级产教融合联盟1个、省级产教融合示范基地2个、省级产教融合工程项目2项。学院成立应用技术研究院、区域经济与社会发展研究院等高水平研究院，获批浙江省智能家电产业大脑、浙江

宁波大学科学技术学院
College of Science and Technology, Ningbo University

省软科学研究基地、宁波市高校协同创新中心、宁波市工业互联网示范平台等科创平台。

College of Science and Technology, Ningbo University (CST-NBU). CST-NBU, established in April 1999, is a full-time regular higher education institution that offers undergraduate degrees and is recognized as a leading independent college nationwide. The college has proactively integrated with the local economy, carving out a distinctive path of industry-education integration and applied transformation. It has received approval for two provincial-level key modern industry colleges, one provincial-level industry-education integration alliance, two provincial-level industry-education integration demonstration bases, and two provincial-level industry-education integration projects. The college has established high-

level research institutes such as the Applied Technology Research Institute and the Regional Economy and Social Development Research Institute. It has been granted several science and innovation platforms, including the Zhejiang Province Smart Home Appliance Industry Brain, the Zhejiang Province Soft Science Research Base, the Ningbo University Collaborative Innovation Center, and the Ningbo Industrial Internet Demonstration Platform.

学校官网（CST-NBU Official Website）：https://www.ndky.edu.cn

宁波东方理工大学（暂名）。一所由社会力量举办、国家重点支持、浙江省和宁波市共同建设的高起点、高水平、国际化的新型研究型大学。由国际知名教育家、中国科学院院士陈十一担任创校校长。学校以卓越的教育、科研和

宁波东方理工大学 Eastern Institute of Technology, Ningbo

创新推动社会发展，并以服务社会为使命，注重基础研究、强化工程技术、突出前沿交叉，形成以理学、工学、信息、商科为主，兼备特色人文社科的学科体系。

Eastern Institute of Technology, Ningbo (Under construction). Eastern Institute of Technology, Ningbo (EIT; tentative), with a high starting point, is poised to emerge as a new type of high-level, international, research-oriented university initiated by social forces and highly supported by the governments of Zhejiang Province and Ningbo City, as well as other social forces. Chen Shiyi, a renowned educator and CAS academician, serves as the founding President of EIT. The university is committed to fostering social development through exceptional education, cutting-edge research, and a culture of innovation. At the heart of EIT's mission is the aspiration to advance economic and social progress of both the region and the nation. To achieve this, the university emphasizes foundational and applied research, propelling advancements in engineering and technology, and highlighting interdisciplinary and impactful research in science, engineering, information technology and business management, supplemented by humanities and social sciences.

学校官网（EIT Official Website）: https://www.eitech.edu.cn

（三）技术研究
Technological Research

截至 2023 年，宁波布局新型产业技术研究院 30 家，集聚科技人才 3 万余名，承担科研项目 1000 多项，孵化科技企业 500 余家[⑥]。主要产业技术研究院如下。

As of 2023, Ningbo has received approval for the establishment of 30 new-generation industrial technology research institutes. These institutes have successfully attracted a talent pool of over 30000 science and technology professionals, who are actively engaged in over 1000 research projects and have facilitated the incubation of more than 500 technology enterprises[⑥]. The major industrial technology institutes are listed below.

中国科学院宁波材料技术与工程研究所。由中国科学院、浙江省人民政府、宁波市人民政府三方共同组建，获批浙江省新型研发机构，围绕材料研究，先后布局材料技术、先进制造、新能源、生物医学

⑥ 资料来源：宁波市科学技术局。
Source: Ningbo Science and Technology Bureau.

4大领域，设立公共测试、专业研发、工程化、先进制造4大类支撑平台，建成中国科学院磁性材料与器件重点实验室等省部级及以上各类平台43个，与

中国科学院宁波材料技术与工程研究所
Ningbo Institute of Materials Technology and Engineering, CAS

国内1500多家企业和全球250多个知名机构开展广泛合作，实现近百项重大科技成果的转移转化。

Ningbo Institute of Materials Technology and Engineering (NIMTE), CAS. NIMTE, a research institute affiliated to CAS, was officially co-founded in 2004 by CAS, Zhejiang provincial government and Ningbo municipal government. As the first state-owned research institute in Zhejiang Province, NIMTE has been devoted to the four fields of materials science: materials technology, advanced manufacturing, new energy, and biomedical engineering and to integrating research and technology with high-tech industrialization. Four major suppor platforms (i.e., public testing, professional R&D, engineering, and advanced manufacturing) have been built up, and in particular, there are 43 scientific research platforms at the national, CAS, as well as the provincial and miniterial level, including the CAS Key Laboratory of Magnetic Materials and Devices. NIMTE has been working in extensive collaboration with over 1500 well-established industries and more than 250 renowned institutions, leading to the significant technology transfer of nearly 100 major technologies in total to enterprises.

宁波工业互联网研究院。宁波市人民政府为部署“产业争先”“科技争投”战略而引进的高能级研究院，主攻工业互联网、智能制造、人工智能等前沿领域，获批“科创中国”创新基地和“浙江省新型研发机构”，2022年获批建设智能制造国家新一代人工智能开放创新平台。累计成功孵化近20家高科技公司，集聚各类高科技人才600余名。

Ningbo Industrial Internet Research Institute. The institute was introduced by the Ningbo municipal government as part of its strategy to lead in industry and technology innovation, primarily focusing on such cutting-edge fields as industrial Internet, smart manufacturing, and artificial intelligence. It has been recognized as a base of "Innovation China" and an initial "Provincial-level New R&D Institutions in Zhejiang". In 2022, it received approval to establish the National Next-Generation Artificial Intelligence Open Innovation Platform for Intelligent Manufacturing. Nearly twenty high-tech companies have emerged from its incubation program,

宁波工业互联网研究院 Ningbo Industrial Internet Research Institute

attracting and nurturing over 600 high-tech talents from various fields.

北京航空航天大学宁波创新研究院。由北京航空航天大学和宁波市人民政府共同组建，获批浙江省新型研发机构、科技资源支撑型创新创业特色载体、精密电磁控制技术与装备浙江省工程研究中心和高速高效磁悬浮机电装备宁波市工程研究中心。聚焦航空、航天、新材料、智能制造、医工交叉等领域，初步建成近 30 个高能级科研平台，与央企和地方企业共建 7 个联合实验室。

Ningbo Institute of Technology (NIT), Beihang University. NIT was jointly set up in Ningbo by Beihang University and Ningbo Municipal Government. It has been approved as a novel research and development institution in Zhejiang Province, a characteristic carrier for scientific and technological resource-supported innovation and entrepreneurship, the Zhejiang Provincial Engineering Research Center of Precision Electromagnetic Control Technology and Equipment, the Ningbo Engineering Research Center of High-speed, and High-efficiency Maglev Electromechanical Equipment. Specializing in aviation, aerospace, new materials, intelligent manufacturing, and the interdisciplinary fields of medical science and engineering, the institute has currently

北京航空航天大学宁波创新研究院
Ningbo Institute of Technology, Beihang University

established seven joint laboratories and nearly 30 high-energy research platforms with national and local state-owned enterprises.

中国机械科学研究总院南方中心。由中国机械科学研究总院集团有限公司和宁波市人民政府共同打造。瞄准高端装备制造领域前沿方向，积极打造国际一流、国内领先的装备制造业创新研发平台，为当地产业转型升级和战略性新兴产业布局提供技术研发、技术服务、产业孵化、人才引育等综合性支撑。

Southern Center of China Academy of Machinery Science and Technology (CAM). The center is a collaborative project between China Academy of Machinery Science and Technology Group and Ningbo Municipal Government. Targeting the forefront of high-end equipment manufacturing, it aspires to create an internationally acclaimed and domestically leading innovation and R&D platform for the equipment manufacturing industry. This platform also aims to provide comprehensive support for the transformation and upgrading of local industries and the strategic layout of emerging industries by offering services

中国机械科学研究总院南方中心
Southern Center of China Academy of Machinery Science and Technology

including technological research and development, technological services, industrial incubation, and talent attraction and breeding.

西北工业大学宁波研究院。由宁波市人民政府与西北工业大学共建，拥有柔性电子、智能芯片、无人航行、民用航天、卫星大数据、工业设计、文遗保护等7个技术中心。柔性电子发光材料团队开发的新一代TADF材料突破国外OLED材料技术对国内面板企业的技术及专利限制，卫星大数据团队承担国家“澳科一号”卫星的研制任务。

Ningbo Research Institute of Northwestern Polytechnical University. Established through a collaboration between the Ningbo municipal government and Northwestern Polytechnical University, this institute comprises seven technology centers specializing in flexible electronics, intelligent chips, unmanned navigation, civil aerospace, satellite big data, industrial design, and cultural heritage protection. Notably, the team focused on flexible electronic light-emitting materials has made significant advancements by pioneering a new generation of TADF emissive

西北工业大学宁波研究院
Ningbo Research Institute of Northwestern Polytechnical University

materials. This breakthrough has overcome the technological and patent limitations on domestic panel enterprises in foreign OLED material technology. Another notable achievement is the Satellite Big Data team, which has taken charge of the development of the national satellite Macao Science 1.

（四）企业创新
Entrepreneurial Innovation

近年来，宁波企业研发机构建设取得突破，石墨烯制造业创新中心获批浙江省首个国家制造业创新中心，另有省级创新中心 4 家、省级技术创新中心 3 家、国家级企业技术中心 44 家。

In recent years, significant strides have been made in the construction of technological innovation centers in Ningbo. Notably, Ningbo Graphene Innovation Center secured approval as Zhejiang Province's inaugural national manufacturing innovation center. Also, there are 4 provincial-level innovation centers, 3 provincial-level technology innovation centers, and 44 national-level enterprise technology centers.

石墨烯制造业创新中心。由中国科学院宁波材料技术与工程研究所牵头建设，2022年获批国家级制造业创新中心，是浙江省迄今唯一的国家制造业创新中心。该中心以石墨烯行业关键共性技术策源地、石墨烯产业技术协同创新新高地、石墨烯产业发展服务新典范为定位，聚焦新能源及新能源汽车、海洋工程、传统产业、电子信息、航空航天、高端装备等领域，已设立9大共性技术平台。

Ningbo Graphene Innovation Center (NGIC). NGIC—established under the leadership of NIMTE, CAS — is a national manufacturing innovation center approved in 2022 and currently the only center of its kind across Zhejiang. Among its missions, the center strives towards a crucial curator of shared technologies in the graphene industry, a novel hub for collaborative innovation in graphene industry technology, and a pioneering model for graphene industry development services. There are nine common technology platforms successfully established, covering new energy and new energy vehicles, marine engineering, traditional industries, electronic information, aerospace, and high-end equipment.

石墨烯制造业创新中心 Ningbo Graphene Innovation Center (NGIC)

开启安居生活

A Livable Place

浙江前洋经济开发区　Zhejiang Qianyang Economic Development Zone

2023年，宁波第14次荣登“中国最具幸福感城市”榜单[7]，并在2022年全国公共服务质量监测中位居第二，公共交通、社会保障、公共教育、医疗服务等领域进入全国前十[8]。宁波的“幸福密码”是什么？答案就藏在万家灯火的温暖、医者仁心的妙手，还有诲人不倦的学堂之中。

Ningbo secured its 14th consecutive place on the list of "China's Happiest Cities"[7] in 2023, and ranked second in the national public service quality assessment in 2022, with public transportation, social security, public education, and healthcare services among the top ten in the country[8]. What is Ningbo's "happiness code"? The answer lies in warm homes, convenient transportation, and excellent healthcare and education.

（一）寻医问诊
Hospitals

在宁波，城市“十分钟健康服务圈”基本形成，全科门诊、中医药门诊、健康管理中心星级化建设实现全覆盖，“云医院”“云诊室”“手机挂号付费”等智慧医疗让越来越多的人体验到优质便利的医疗服务。

In Ningbo, the "Ten-Minute Health Service Circle" is now well-established, with star-rated development covering general out-patient clinics, TCM (Traditional Chinese Medicine) out-patient clinics, and health management centers. The implementation of smart solutions such as "online medical services" and "online registration" has further enhanced the accessibility of high-quality and convenient healthcare services to the wider public.

综合性医院。宁波现有5家三甲综合性医院，分别是宁波市医疗中心李惠利医院、宁波大学附属第一医院（宁波市第一医院）、宁波市第二医院、宁波大学附属人民医院（鄞州人民医院）和解放军第906医院。宁波大学附属

⑦ 资料来源：新华社《瞭望东方周刊》、瞭望智库，《2023年度中国最具幸福感城市（省会及计划单列市）》。
Source: 2023 List of China's Happiest Cities, released by Xinhua News Agency's Oriental Outlook Weekly and Liaowang Institution.

⑧ 资料来源：国家市场监管总局，《2022年全国公共服务质量监测情况通报》。
Source: 2022 National Public Service Quality Survey Report, released by State Administration for Market Regulation.

第一医院设有国际门诊部。

General Hospitals. Ningbo has five 3A (the highest of China's three-tier grading system) hospitals, namely, Ningbo Medical Center Lihuili Hospital, the First Affiliated Hospital of Ningbo University (Ningbo No. 1 Hospital), Ningbo No. 2 Hospital, the Affiliated People's Hospital of Ningbo University (Yinzhou People's Hospital), and the People's Liberation Army (PLA) No. 906 Hospital. An international outpatient clinic is established at the First Affiliated Hospital of Ningbo University.

国际门诊部地点：宁波市柳汀街59号，2号楼2楼18号诊室

Clinic location: Room 18, 2nd Floor, Building 2, 59 Liuting Street, Haishu District, Ningbo.

工作时间：周一至周六8：00—11：30，14：00—17：00

Opening hours: Monday to Saturday 8:00-11:30, 14:00-17:00

预约电话：（0574）87085080　手机号码：13884456860

Appointment telephone: +86-574-87085080　Mobile: +86 13884456860

专业特色医院。宁波有6家三甲专业特色医院，分别是宁波大学附属妇女儿童医院、宁波市中医院、宁波市眼科医院、宁波大学附属康宁医院、宁波市第六医院和宁波市奉化区中医医院。

Special Hospitals. Ningbo also owns six 3A special hospitals, namely, Ningbo Women & Children's Hospital, Ningbo Municipal Hospital of Traditional Chinese Medicine, Ningbo Eye Hospital, the Affiliated Kangning Hospital of Ningbo University, Ningbo No. 6 Hospital, and Fenghua District Hospital of Traditional Chinese Medicine.

宁波市三级甲等医院清单（截至 2024 年 1 月）

三甲医院	类型	地址	服务热线
宁波市医疗中心李惠利医院	综合医院	兴宁院区：兴宁路 57 号	0574-87018701
		东部院区：江南路 1111 号	0574-55835583
宁波大学附属第一医院（宁波市第一医院）	综合医院	月湖院区：柳汀街 59 号	0574-87085588
		方桥院区：机场南路 1601 号	0574-87085030
		外滩院区：人民路 247 号	0574-87035399
宁波市第二医院	综合医院	本部院区：西北街 41 号	0574-83870999
		北部院区：永丰北路 175 号	0574-87089581
宁波大学附属人民医院（鄞州人民医院）	综合医院	百丈东路 251 号	0574-87016888
解放军第 906 医院（原 113 医院）	综合医院	中山东路 337 号	0574-27754000
宁波大学附属妇女儿童医院	妇幼保健	南部院区：柳汀街 339 号	0574-87083300
		北部院区：慈城新城慈水西街 266 号	0574-87651741
宁波市中医院	中医医院	总院：丽园北路 819 号	0574-87089035
		鄞州分院：天童北路 170 号	—
宁波大学附属康宁医院	精神专科医院	庄市：庄俞南路 1 号	0574-26251111
		海曙：范江岸路 1105 号	0574-26252222
		鄞州：百丈东路 926 号	0574-26253333
宁波市眼科医院	眼科医院	北明程路 599 号	0574-87739000
宁波市第六医院	骨科医院	中山东路 1059 号	0574-87660660
宁波市奉化区中医医院	中医医院	奉化区岳林街道金海路 462 号	0574-88586008

List of 3A Hospitals in Ningbo (As of Jan. 2024)

3A Hospital	Type	Address	Hotline
Ningbo Medical Center Lihuili Hospital	General hospital	Xingning Branch: 57 Xingning Road	+86-574-87018701
		Dongbu Branch: 1111 Jiangnan Road	+86-574-55835583
The First Affiliated Hospital of Ningbo University	General hospital	Yuehu Branch: 59 Liuting Street	+86-574-87085588
		Fangqiao Branch: 1601 South Airport Road	+86-574-87085030
		Waitan Branch: 247 Renmin Road	+86-574-87035399
Ningbo No. 2 Hospital	General hospital	Main Campus: 41 Northwest Street	+86-574-83870999
		North Campus: 175 Yongfeng North Road	+86-574-87089581
The Affiliated People's Hospital of Ningbo University (Yinzhou People's Hospital)	General hospital	251 Baizhang East Road	+86-574-87016888
PLA No. 906 Hospital (the former PLA No. 113 Hospital)	General hospital	337 Zhongshan East Road	+86-574-27754000
Ningbo Women & Children's Hospital	Maternal and child health care	South Section: 339 Liuting Street	+86-574-87083300
		North Section: 266 Cishui West Street, Cicheng New City	+86-574-87651741
Ningbo Municipal Hospital of Traditional Chinese Medicine	TCM hospital	Main Campus: 819 Liyuan North Road	+86-574-87089035
		Yinzhou Branch: 170 Tiantong North Road	—
The Affiliated Kangning Hospital of Ningbo University	Psychiatric hospital	Zhuangshi Branch: 1 Zhuangyu South Road	+86-574-26251111
		Haishu Branch: 1105 Fan Jiangan Road	+86-574-26252222
		Yinzhou Branch: 926 Baizhang East Road	+86-574-26253333
Ningbo Eye Hospital	Eye hospital	599 North Mingcheng Road	+86-574-87739000
Ningbo No. 6 Hospital	Orthopedic hospital	1059 Zhongshan East Road, Yinzhou District	+86-574-87660660
Fenghua District Hospital of Traditional Chinese Medicine	TCM hospital	462 Jinhai Road, Yuelin Street, Fenghua District	+86-574-88586008

外籍人员医保。在甬就业的外籍人员参加职工基本医疗保险，由用人单位提供外籍人员的护照、外国人就业证或外国人专家证等就业证明即可参保；在甬居住但未就业的外籍人员，可以凭外国人永久居留证参加宁波城乡居民基本医疗保险，其中具有全日制学籍的外籍留学生，可在宁波各所学校以学生的身份参加城乡居民基本医保。参加职工医保或城乡居民基本医保的，按照参保类型享受基本医保待遇。

Expatriate medical insurance. Foreign nationals employed in Ningbo are eligible to participate in the basic medical insurance for employees. Employers are required to provide employment certificates such as passports, Foreigner's Work Permit, or Foreign Expert Certificate for the enrollment process. Foreign nationals residing in Ningbo but not employed can participate in the urban and rural residents' basic medical insurance with their Foreign Permanent Resident ID Cards. Full-time international students in Ningbo institutions can join the basic medical insurance under their student identity. Insured individuals will receive corresponding benefits based on their insurance type.

宁波市公众健康服务平台（网址：https://www.nbgzjk.cn）
The Public Health Service Platform of Ningbo (Website: https://www.nbgzjk.cn)

挂号热线：0574-55012320　咨询热线：0574-55001200
Appointment Hotline: +86-574-55012320　Consulting Hotline: +86-574-55001200

预约挂号等医疗服务可关注“健康宁波”微信公众号：health_ningbo
Appointment via WeChat: Follow "Health Ningbo" (ID: health_ningbo)

（二）学无止境
Schooling

在宁波，教育事业蓬勃发展。宁波素有“文教之邦”的美誉，尤其是基础教育走在全国前列。截至 2023 年，宁波拥有幼儿园 949 所、小学 381 所、初中 250 所、中职学校 32 所、普通高中 88 所[⑨]。

Thanks to its flourishing educational endeavors, Ningbo is widely acclaimed as the "City of Culture and Education". Its basic education is at the forefront nationwide. As of 2023, Ningbo runs a total of 949 kindergartens, 381 elementary schools, 250 junior high schools, 32 secondary vocational schools, and 88 senior high schools[⑨].

外籍人员子女在宁波就学，可以选择入读浙江宁波乔治亚外籍人员子女学校、浙江宁波英伦外籍人员子女学校或浙江宁波协和外籍人员子女学校。这三所学校是 K12 一贯制学校，涵盖了从幼儿园到高中的全链条教育服务。

Children of expatriates in Ningbo can choose to attend Georgia School (GSN), Ningbo British International School (NBIS), or Concordia International School Ningbo (CISN). These schools are K-12 integrated system schools, offering educational services from kindergarten to high school.

宁波市镇海中学　Ningbo Zhenhai High School

宁波市的高中在全国享有盛誉，为海内外高校输送了大量优秀人才。镇海中学每年有

⑨ 资料来源：宁波市教育局。
Source: Ningbo Education Bureau.

10% 左右的毕业生被清华大学、北京大学录取，效实中学曾培养出童第周、屠呦呦等杰出人才。

High schools in Ningbo are renowned nationwide, having sent a wealth of talents to colleges and universities at home and abroad. For instance, around 10% of graduates from Zhenhai High School are admitted to top Chinese universities such as

Tsinghua University and Peking University each year. Xiaoshi High School has also cultivated numerous outstanding individuals, including the renowned embryologist T.C. Tung and Nobel Prize laureate in Physiology or Medicine, Tu Youyou.

（三）出行指南
Travel

在宁波，机场高铁、轨道交通、骑行步道等城市交通体系密织成网。根据百度地图发布的《2023 年度中国城市交通报告》，在 100 个重点城市中，宁波在“公共交通出行中的平均步行距离短”榜单中排第 9 位。

Ningbo's urban transportation system, comprising the airport, high-speed rail, metro, cycling paths, and pedestrian walkways, is intricately woven into a comprehensive network. The report of "2023 Urban Public Transport in China" released by Baidu Maps reveals that among 100 major Chinese cities, Ningbo ranked 9th on the list of "shorter walking trips to local public transport stops".

宁波栎社国际机场。中国境内重要的区域枢纽机场、国际（地区）定期航班机场、对外开放的一类航空口岸，与中国主要城市均开通直航，国际航班也在不断扩增中。市内交通便利，地铁 2 号线可直达机场。

宁波栎社国际机场　Ningbo Lishe International Airport

Ningbo Lishe International Airport. This important regional hub airport in China serves as a CAT I aviation port open to international (regional) flights. Its direct flights are available to all major cities in China and its international flights are expanding. Its convenient access to the city center of Ningbo is readily available, with Metro Line 2 offering direct connections.

宁波栎社国际机场客运通航城市和地区

国内城市	北京、上海、广州、深圳、成都、长沙、阜阳、揭阳、泸州、石家庄、武汉、郑州、重庆、哈尔滨、昆明、青岛、大连、海口、赣州、井冈山、绵阳、太原、西安、兰州、三亚、宜宾、珠海、长春、贵阳、景德镇、天津、西昌、宜昌、遵义、桂林、库车、南宁、铜仁、西宁、宜春、安庆、郴州、万州、西双版纳、襄阳、银川、巴中、毕节、衡阳、丽江、厦门、威海、兴义、鄂州、淮安、临沂、沈阳、乌鲁木齐、烟台、运城、安康、湘西、营口
港澳台地区	香港、澳门、台北
国际城市	新加坡、东京、大阪、济州、布达佩斯

Passenger Cities and areas of Ningbo Lishe International Airport

Domestic	Beijing, Shanghai, Guangzhou, Shenzhen, Chengdu, Changsha, Fuyang, Jieyang, Luzhou, Shijiazhuang, Wuhan, Zhengzhou, Chongqing, Harbin, Kunming, Qingdao, Dalian, Haikou, Ganzhou, Jinggangshan, Mianyang, Taiyuan, Xi'an, Lanzhou, Sanya, Yibin, Zhuhai, Changchun, Guiyang, Jingdezhen, Tianjin, Xichang, Yichang, Zunyi, Guilin, Kuqa, Nanning, Tongren, Xining, Yichun, Anqing, Chenzhou, Wanzhou, Xishuangbanna, Xiangyang, Yinchuan, Bazhong, Bijie, Hengyang, Lijiang, Xiamen, Weihai, Xingyi, Ezhou, Huai'an, Linyi, Shenyang, Urumqi, Yantai, Yuncheng, Ankang, Xiangxi, Yingkou
Hong Kong, Macau, Taiwan	Hong Kong, Macau, Taipei
International	Singapore,Tokyo, Osaka, Jeju, Budapest

宁波栎社国际机场出租车及网约车乘车点

出租车乘车点	1 号航站楼 1 楼到达层 14 号门外
	2 号航站楼 1 楼到达层 22 号门外
网约车乘车点	1 号航站楼到达层 14 号门出向前约 100 米
	2 号航站楼国内、国际到达出，根据指引乘坐扶梯、电梯到达地铁通道。沿通道直行约 50 米，右转进入 B2 层 F 区的上车点

Pick–up Points for Taxi and Ride–hailing

Pick-up Points for Taxi	Terminal 1: Outside Gate 14 of Arrival Hall, 1st Floor
	Terminal 2: Outside Gate 22 of Arrival Hall, 1st Floor
Pick-up Points for Ride-hailing	Terminal 1: 100 meters from Gate 14 of Arrival Hall, 1st Floor
	Terminal 2: For both domestic and international arrivals, follow the guidelines to take the escalator or elevator to the subway passage. Continue straight for about 50 meters, then turn right to enter the pick-up point in Zone F on level B2

宁波铁路运输。截至 2023 年，宁波铁路网运营总里程超过 400 千米，是中国 50 个铁路枢纽之一[10]。未来拟建成通苏嘉甬铁路、甬舟铁路、甬金铁路等。从宁波出发乘坐高铁，1 小时可到达杭州，2 小时可抵达上海，7 小时可达北京，8.5 小时可达深圳。

Ningbo Railway Transportation. By 2023, Ningbo's railway network has spaned a total operating mileage of 400 kilometers, making it one of China's 50 railway hubs[10]. Future plans include the construction of high-speed railways such as Nantong-Suzhou-Jiaxing-Ningbo, Ningbo-Zhoushan, and Ningbo-Jinhua lines. Departing from Ningbo by high-speed train, you can reach Hangzhou in 1 hour, Shanghai in 2 hours, Beijing in 7 hours, and Shenzhen in 8.5 hours.

中国铁路 12306 网站：https://www.12306.cn/index/

Website of 12306 China Railway: https://www.12306.cn/en/index.html

服务热线：12306

Service Hotline: +86 12306

官方 App 下载：

Official App:

⑩ 资料来源：宁波市交通运输局。
Source: Ningbo Municipal Transport Bureau.

宁波火车站 Ningbo Railway Station

宁波轨道交通。宁波第一条轨道交通线路于 2014 年 5 月开通试运营。十年来，宁波相继开通运营轨道 1 号线、2 号线、3 号线一期、4 号线和 5 号线一期，其中 5 号线是浙江省首条全自动运行线路。截至 2023 年，宁波轨道交通运营总里程达 186 千米，基本实现对主城区的覆盖 ⑪。未来，宁波远期规划 16 条线路，总规模约 1157 千米，逐步形成市域 60 分钟交通圈 ⑫。

Ningbo Metro. Ningbo launched its first metro line in 2014. The past decade witnessed the inauguration of Lines 1, 2, 3 (Phase 1), 4, and 5 (Phase 1); in

⑪ 资料来源：宁波市轨道交通集团有限公司。
Source: Ningbo Rail Transit Group Co. Ltd.
⑫ 资料来源：《宁波市轨道交通线网规划（2021–2035 年）》。
Source: 2021–2035 Construction Plan of Ningbo Rail Transit.

particular, Line 5 is the first fully automated metro route in Zhejiang Province. As of 2023, its rail transit system has reached a total operating mileage of 186 km, effectively covering the main urban areas[11]. In the future, Ningbo plans to develop 16 lines, with a total length of about 1157 km, gradually building a 60-minute traffic circle[12].

宁波轨道交通　Ningbo Rail Transit

宁波轨道交通运营线网示意图
Ningbo Rail Transit System Map

宁波轨道交通运营线网示意图 Ningbo Rail Transit System Map

“宁波轨道交通”官方微信

WeChat Official Account of "Ningbo Metro"

其他市内交通。宁波推动轨道、公交与慢行交通三网融合，塑造了生态友好、文明友善的城市绿色出行体系。截至 2023 年，宁波公交标准运营车辆 9772.9 台，运营线路 1243 条，运营总里程 4.7 万千米；全市巡游出租车 6205 辆；公共自行车网点 900 个，公共自行车 17500 辆[13]。

Alternative Local Transportation Options. Ningbo promotes the integration of rail transit, buses, and slow modes of transportation (cycling + walking), shaping an eco-friendly and civilized transportation system. By the end of 2023, the city has boasted a fleet of 9772.9 standard buses operating on 1243 routes, covering a total distance of 47000 kilometers. It also has 6205 registered taxicabs, 23000+ online ride-hailing vehicles, 900 public bicycle stations, and a total of 17500 public bicycles[13].

⑬ 资料来源：宁波市交通运输局。
Source: Ningbo Municipal Transport Bureau.

篇章三
Chapter Three

都市乐活，人间烟火

City of True Happiness

宁波东部新城生态走廊　Ecological corridor, Ningbo Eastern New Town

宁波是一座古老又年轻的城市，融合了历史文化的深厚底蕴和现代都市的蓬勃活力。

Ningbo is a city that seamlessly combines rich historical roots with a vibrant modern urban energy.

若醉心自然，则驾一叶扁舟，徜徉山水间，看八百里四明山绵延，看三江六塘河水润甬城。

If you have a passion for nature, immerse yourself in the beauty of its landscape — behold Siming Mountains stretching hundreds of miles and water ways weaving through the entire city.

若好访古迹，则叩开天一阁的门扉，或探寻河姆渡文化的久远。

If you embrace much enthusiasm for history, unlock the doors of Tianyi Pavilion and delve into the ancient roots of Hemudu culture.

若爱好文艺，博物馆、城市书房、各大剧场等你发现精彩。

If you are keen on arts and culture, explore the wonders in its museums, 24-hour city's studies, and various theaters.

若品尝美食，海鲜大餐、新鲜蔬果、糕点小吃在桌上一字排开。

If you are a culinary connoisseur, a feast of seafood, fresh fruits, and a delightful array of pastries and snacks awaits your palate.

若喜爱运动，各类健身项目、丰富的户外运动、多元赛事活动总有一款适合你。

If you love sports, a range of fitness facilities, diverse outdoor activities, and numerous sporting events are all set for you to enjoy.

若需要购物，从普通商品到奢侈品，从手工艺品到家具百货，总能满足你的消费需求。

If shopping is on your agenda, there is always something to meet your needs, from everyday items to luxury goods, from handicrafts to furniture.

欢度假日时光

Getaway Places

四明湖水杉　Metasequoia Woods, Siming Lake

宁波具有海丝文化、海天佛国、海湾风情、海鲜美味以及瓷韵、帆韵、禅韵、茶韵的“四海四韵”滨海旅游新特色，从雪窦山到象山影视城，从余姚的河姆渡遗址到北仑的东方大港，从鄞江它山堰到贯穿全市的三江六塘河，每一个角落都散发着浓厚的地方特色和独特的文化韵味。欢迎“顺着运河来看海，伴着书香游宁波”。

Ningbo showcases a coastal allure with features like the Maritime Silk Road culture, the Buddhist wonderland, picturesque coastal scenery, and delectable seafood. Simultaneously, it embraces elements with a distinct Chinese charm, including "ceramics, sailing, Chinese Chan (aka. Zen), and tea". From Mount Xuedou to Xiangshan Global Studios, from Yuyao Hemudu Site to Beilun Port, from Tuoshan Weir to the city water ways, every corner exudes strong local characteristics and unique cultural flavor.

（一）寻山问水
Outing and Hiking

宁波是“三江六塘河，一湖居其中”的宜居城市，是中国大运河南端出海口、“海上丝绸之路”东方始发港，枕山、滨海、拥江、揽湖是宁波特有的地理格局和资源特色。

Ningbo, a city known for its livability, is blessed with a distinctive geographical layout, abundant natural resources, and a harmonious blend of three great rivers, meandering canals, and the peaceful Moon Lake. As the southern terminus of the Grand Canal of China and the gateway to the Maritime Silk Road, this enchanting city beautifully combines rugged mountains, sparkling seas, and the tranquil embrace of rivers and lakes.

雪窦山——中国五大佛教名山之一。国家 5A 级旅游景区，国家级风景名胜区，国家森林公园，平均海拔 800 米，以剡水、古刹和幽谷飞瀑闻名遐迩，有“海上蓬莱，陆上天台”之美誉。雪窦山上的雪窦寺拥有世界最高的坐姿铜制露天弥勒大佛造像，弥勒圣坛成为宁波文化旅游新地标。

Mount Xuedou: A top 5 buddhist mountain in China. Mount Xuedou is a national 5A-level tourist attraction with an average altitude of 800 meters. Renowned for

雪窦山 Mount Xuedou

the Shanxi River, Xuedou Temple, and tempting waterfalls, it is praised as the "Fairyland on the Sea". Xuedou Temple boasts the world's tallest seated bronze Buddha Maitreya in the open. Its Maitreya Sanctuary has emerged as a new cultural and tourist landmark in Ningbo.

四明山——“天然氧吧”“避暑胜地”。分布在宁波市西部的余姚、海曙西南和奉化，平均海拔 700 米，有着“第二庐山”美誉，诗人李白等曾为四明山美景纵情吟咏。

Siming Mountains: "Nature's Oxygen Bar" and "Escape from the Summer Heat." Situated in the western part of Ningbo (including Yuyao, southwestern Haishu,

四明湖　Siming Lake

四明山　Siming Mountains

and Fenghua), Siming Mountains – with an average elevation of 700 meters – is acclaimed as the "Second Mount Lu." Renowned poets like Li Bai have praised and extolled its captivating beauty.

月湖——宁波宋韵文化集中展示地。国家5A级旅游景区，因宽处像满月、狭处如眉月而得名。宋元年间建成的月湖十洲，成为浙东学术中心，是文人墨客憩息荟萃之地。北宋名臣王安石、南宋宰相史浩、宋代著名学者杨简、明末清初大史学家万斯同等风流人物都曾在月湖或隐居、或讲学、或为官、或著书。

月湖 Moon Lake

月湖 Moon Lake

Moon Lake: Reflecting the local charm of the Song Dynasty. As a national 5A-level tourist attraction, the lake stands at the center of Ningbo, named for its resemblance to a full moon at its widest and a crescent moon at its narrowest. During the Song and Yuan Dynasties, the construction of ten islets in the lake established it as an academic center of East Zhejiang and a favored gathering place for literati. A number of prominent figures from Chinese history took residence, delivered lectures, held official posts, or wrote books here. Among them, you can find Wang Anshi, a renowned minister of the Southern Song Dynasty; Shi Hao, a chancellor of the Southern Song Dynasty; Yang Jian, a famous scholar of the Southern Song Dynasty; and Wan Sitong, a great historian from the late Ming and early Qing dynasties.

东钱湖——浙江省最大的天然淡水湖。国家级旅游度假区和国家体育旅游示范基地，被郭沫若先生誉为“西湖风光，太湖气魄”，集聚了宋韵文化、佛教文化等文化基因。环湖有小普陀、马山休闲旅游区等景区景点以及单车驿站、帆船基地、高尔夫度假村等体育休闲地，拥有步行、舟行、骑行、车行“四行东钱湖”大众休闲产品。

东钱湖 Dongqian Lake

Dongqian Lake: Zhejiang Province's magnificent freshwater gem. This gem is not only the largest natural freshwater lake in the province but also a nationally recognized tourist resort, showcasing the perfect blend of West Lake's elegance and Taihu Lake's grandeur. As the renowned Chinese literary figure Guo Moruo once praised, Dongqian Lake is filled with cultural heritage that embodies the charm of the Song Dynasty, the wisdom of wealth culture, and the influence of Buddhism. Surrounding the lake, you'll discover captivating attractions like the Small Putuo Scenic Area and the Mashan Wetland, as well as various sports and leisure facilities, including bicycle stations, sailing bases, and golf resorts. Embarking on a journey around this picturesque destination can be experienced through walking, boating, cycling, or driving, providing endless opportunities for exploration and enjoyment.

梅山湾——集海洋、文化、旅游、体育于一体的滨海旅游度假区。浙江

梅山湾 Meishan Bay

省级旅游度假区，拥有中国港口博物馆、梅山湾沙滩公园、宁波国际赛道、梅山湾冰雪大世界、万博鱼体育旅游度假区、梅山红桥等核心旅游景点，汇集海洋主题游乐、体育运动休闲、文化研学旅游等多元业态于一体。

Meishan Bay: A coastal reort integrating ocean, culture, tourism and sports. This provincial-level resort features tourist attractions such as China Port Museum, Meishan Bay Beach Park, Ningbo International Speedpark, Meishan Bay Ice and Snow World, Wanboofish Resort, Meishan Red Bridge, etc. Here you can find the blend of diverse formats such as marine-themed amusement, sports and leisure activities, and educational tourism.

宁波湾——全宁波近郊唯一的蓝色海湾。浙江省级旅游度假区，是宁波少有的蓝海片区，东海的三大著名渔港之一，被联合国开发计划署授予“绿色发展中国试点”。度假区集聚高端酒店、商业街区、渔人码头、精品赛事等资源

宁波湾天妃湖 Tianfei Lake (Ningbo Bay, Fenghua)

共同打造“运动之海、休闲之湾”。

Ningbo Bay: The only blue bay in the entire outskirts of Ningbo. As a provincial-level resort in Zhejiang, the bay represents one of the scarce blue sea areas in Ningbo. It stands as one of the three renowned fishing ports in the East China Sea, and recognized as the "Pilot Project of Green Development in China" by the United Nations Development Program (UNDP). This resort perfectly blends upscale hotels, bustling commercial streets, scenic wharves, and exciting sporting events, creating a destination renowned for its tagline "Sports by the Sea, Leisure by the Bay".

大目湾——拥有枕山滨海独特资源优势。周边有松兰山旅游度假区（2022年杭州亚运会帆船赛事举办地）、阿拉的海水上乐园等一批滨海旅游区

大目湾　Damu Bay

域。大目湾新城将建设成为具有一流滨海风情，集海洋景观、海上运动、养生康疗、休闲度假、时尚居住于一体的滨海休闲新城。

Damu Bay: Boasting unique resource advantages with mountains and sea in close proximity. The surrounding region features a cluster of coastal tourist destinations, including the Songlanshan Tourist Resort (venue for the sailing events of the 2022 Hangzhou Asian Games) and Our Sea Water Park. The Damu Bay New Town will be developed into a first-class coastal area, integrating marine landscapes, water sports, health and wellness therapies, leisure vacations, and stylish living.

（二）寻古探今
Places of Interest

宁波是国家历史文化名城，是中华文明的重要发源地和书藏古今的书香之城。古往今来的治水壮举、建筑奇迹，对内的文化沉淀、对外的文化交流，处处体现着文化厚度和世界影响力。

In 1986, Ningbo was honored with the prestigious title of being a national-level historical and cultural city in China. With its rich history and deep cultural roots, Ningbo stands as a cradle of Chinese civilization. The city boasts a legacy of literary traditions, architectural marvels, and remarkable accomplishments in water management, all of which contribute to its cultural depth and significant global influence.

天一阁——中国现存最早的图书馆，亚洲现存最早的私家藏书楼。国家5A级旅游景区，至今已有460多年历史，以藏书文化为特色，融社会历史、艺术于一体，是中国重点文物保护单位。博物馆内环境幽雅、园林精美、建筑古朴，富有浓郁的地方特色，除了藏书丰富，其建筑结构在防火、通风、防潮方面也独具特色。

Tianyige Library: The oldest extant library in China as well as the most ancient private library across Asia. With a history of over 460 years, this national 5A-level tourist attraction blends social history and art, featuring its enormous collection of rare ancient books and documents. It has been on the list of cultural heritage sites under state protection. Tianyige Library Museum – rich in local characters – offers an elegant environment, with its exquisite gardens and quaint

天一阁 Tianyige Library

architecture. In addition to the extensive collection of books, its architectural structure is uniquely designed for fire prevention, ventilation, and moisture control.

河姆渡遗址——长江流域是中华文明发源地的重要见证。1973 年首次发现，1982 年被列为全国重点文物保护单位，2021 年入选中国“百年百大考古发现”。

河姆渡遗址附近的井头山遗址，是长三角地区首个贝丘遗址，是迄今为止中国沿海发现的埋藏最深、年代最早的典型海岸贝丘遗址，把宁波的人文历史源头又向前推进了1000多年。目前，宁波正在建设河姆渡国家考古遗址公园。

Hemudu Cultural Site: Consolidating Yangtze River Basin as an important birthplace of Chinese civilization. Unearthed in 1973, it was listed as an important heritage site under state protection in 1982, and selected as one of China's "100 Centurial Archaeological Discoveries" in 2021. The Jingtoushan site near the Hemudu site is the first shell mound in the Yangtze River Delta region and the deepest buried and oldest coastal shell mound site that China has found so far. The cultural and historical roots of Ningbo have been extended over a thousand years further. The Hemudu National Archaeological Site Park is currently under construction.

它山堰——中国古代四大水利工程之一。全国重点文物保护单位，中国水利史上首次出现的块石砌筑的重力型拦河滚水坝，2015年入选世界灌溉工

河姆渡遗址　Hemudu Cultural Site

它山堰　Tuoshan Weir

程遗产名单，与郑国渠、灵渠、都江堰合称为中国古代四大水利工程。

Tuoshan Weir: One of China's Four Great Ancient Water Conservancy Projects. As a nationally protected cultural relic, this gravity overflow dam constructed with block stones holds the distinction of being the first of its kind in the history of Chinese water conservancy. In 2015, it was included in the World Heritage Irrigation Structure list, alongside Zhengguo Canal, Lingqu Canal, and Dujiangyan Irrigation System. Together, these remarkable structures form the cornerstone of ancient Chinese water conservancy achievements.

慈城古县城——江南地区保存最完整的千年古县城。国家 4A 级旅游景区、国家历史文化名镇、中国慈孝文化之乡，中国民族优秀建筑文化遗产名镇和旅游目的地。"慈城古建筑群"被列为全国重点文物保护单位。游客在城

慈城古县城 Cicheng Ancient County

内可以体验特色民宿、江南小吃、非遗民俗等。

Cicheng Ancient County: The most well-preserved millennial county in the Jiangnan region. This well-known historical and cultural town is listed as a national 4A-level tourist attraction. Renowned for its filial piety culture, this attraction with fascinating architectural relics is an ideal tourist destination. The "Cicheng Ancient Architectural Complex" is under state-level protection. Tourists will be satisfied with distinctive lodgings, local snacks and intangible cultural heritage among others.

天童寺　Tiantong Temple

天童寺——佛教禅宗五大名刹之一。全国重点文物保护单位，号称“东南佛国”，是宁波人的礼佛圣地。宋元时期佛教东传之路便以天童为起点，沿海丝之路传往东瀛，是古代中国禅宗东传中心。每年秋季，天童寺进入银杏最佳观赏期。

Tiantong Temple: One of the five sacred Chinese Chan Buddhist temples. Tiantong Temple, referred to as the "Southeast Buddhist Kingdom", is a national key protected cultural relic unit and a holy place for Ningbonese to worship Buddha. During the Song and Yuan dynasties, the route for the eastward spread of Buddhism began at Tiantong Temple and followed the Maritime Silk Road to Japan. The temple stands as the hub for the spread of Chinese Chan Buddhism to the East. Visitors can revel in the mesmerizing beauty of the temple's gingko trees, especially during the enchanting autumn season.

保国寺——长江以南最古老、保存最完整的木结构建筑之一。国家4A级旅游景区、全国重点文物保护单位，寺内的大雄宝殿（又称无梁殿）是被称为“江南一绝”的古建筑瑰宝，唐、宋、元、明、清、民国的建筑各有特色，是中国建筑文化发展的一部活史书。

Baoguo Temple: One of the oldest and best-preserved wooden structures in the region south of the Yangtze River. Baoguo Temple is another national 4A-level tourist attraction and a national key protected cultural relic unit. Mahavira Hall or Grand Hall (aka. No-Beam Hall) in the temple is one of the best ancient architectural treasures in the region south of the Yangtze River. The architecture there presents striking features of the Tang, Song, Yuan, Ming, Qing Dynasties and the Republican periods, unfolding a physical history of Chinese architectural culture.

（三）寻梦环游
Theme Parks

以文化体验为特色的影视城、以科普教育为特色的动植物园、以遛娃

保国寺 Baoguo Temple

消遣为特色的儿童公园、以数字文化为特色的主题乐园、以生态保护为特色的湿地公园……功能各异的休闲娱乐好去处，总有一款适合你和你的家人。

Film and television studios, zoos and botanical gardens, children's parks, amusement parks, and wetland parks have been developed to provide opportunities for cultural immersion, education, entertainment, and ecological conservation. The following multifunctional theme parks offer diverse leisure and recreational options, catering to the interests and enjoyment of visitors.

象山影视城——中国十大影视基地之一。国家 4A 级旅游景区，以灵岩山为大背景，打造中国首个实景电影主题乐园，曾有《神雕侠侣》等 1500 多部影视作品相继在此拍摄。

象山影视城 Xiangshan Global Studios

Xiangshan Global Studios: One of "China's Top 10 Film and TV Bases". Located in Xinqiao town, Xiangshan county, the national 4A-level tourist attraction is China's first live film theme park set in Lingyan Mountain. Sincc its opening in 2005, over 1500 films and TV series including *Divine Condor, Errant Knight* have been shot here.

宁波野生动物园——中国水域面积较大的野生动物园。国家 4A 级旅游景区，汇集动物 300 余种、万余只（头），首创国内动物园水上观赏动物游线。

Ningbo Wildlife Park:China's Premier Aquatic Wildlife Destination. As a nationally recognized 4A-level tourist attraction, Ningbo Wildlife Park captivates visitors with its immense aquatic area, offering an exciting and immersive experience like no other. This pioneering park boasts the first-ever water-based viewing route in China, allowing visitors to marvel at about 10000 animals from over 300 diverse species.

宁波野生动物园 Ningbo Wildlife Park

宁波植物园　Ningbo Botanical Garden

宁波植物园——一座兼具生态景观和植物科学文化内涵的植物园。分为体育休闲植物区、科普观光植物区和花卉园艺植物区三大片区，具有科普、旅游、休闲等综合功能。

Ningbo Botanical Garden: A botanical garden integrating ecological landscape and botanical sciences. The botanical garden is divided into three areas, namely, sport leisure area, popular science and sightseeing area, and flower and gardening area. The three areas serve for ecology, science popularizing, tourism and leisure purposes.

宁波方特主题乐园　Ningbo Fantawild Theme Park

宁波方特主题乐园——大型高科技第四代主题乐园。包括东方神话（国家 4A 级旅游景区）与东方欲晓两个主题乐园。东方神话设有民间传说、民间戏曲、神秘文化等八类项目。东方欲晓以百余年来中华民族的奋斗历程为背景，游客在此可以获得“红色旅游新体验”。

Ningbo Fantawild Theme Park: A large 4th generation hi-tech theme park. It includes two theme parks, Oriental Heritage (listed as a national 4A-level tourist attraction) and Glorious Orient. The former has 8 programs including folklore, folk opera, and mysterious culture. The latter one focuses on the theme of the Chinese nation's struggle throughout the past century, providing visitors with a unique and

杭州湾国家湿地公园 Hangzhou Bay National Wetland Park

immersive experience of Red Tourism, which involves traveling to historical sites with a revolutionary legacy in China.

杭州湾国家湿地公园——浙江十大“最美湿地”之一。属于典型的海岸湿地生态系统，是在全球环境基金（GEF）和世界银行合作支持下的东亚海陆源污染消减基金的第一个项目，是集湿地恢复、湿地研究和环境教育于一体的湿地生态保护和旅游区。

Hangzhou Bay National Wetland Park: One of the top ten "Most Beautiful Wetlands" in Zhejiang. Hangzhou Bay wetlands as a typical coastal wetland ecosystem is the first project of East Asia Land-Based Pollution Reduction Investment Fund supported by Global Environment Facility (GEF) and World Bank. The wetland park serves as an ecological preservation and tourism area that integrates wetland restoration and research, and environmental education.

（四）寻乡觅趣
Beautiful Villages

在“千村示范、万村整治”工程的引领下，宁波A级景区村覆盖率超过62%[①]，成为“吃住行游购娱”全产业要素集聚的乡村微度假旅游目的地。文艺打卡、民俗体验、民宿度假、运动休闲、红色教育……可以满足您的多样需求。

As Zhejiang province advances the Green Rural Revival Program, over 62% villages in Ningbo are ranked among A-level scenic villages[①]. These villages have become ideal micro-vacation destinations where visitors have access to food, accommodation, transportation, tourism, shopping and entertainment. The captivating villages can meet tourists' various needs such as visiting popular tourist spots, experiencing folklore, taking vacations in B&B, enjoying sports and leisure, and receiving "red education" on the history of revolution.

滕头村——中国生态第一村。国家5A级旅游景区，以“生态农业”“立体农业”“碧水、蓝天”绿化工程，形成别具一格的生态旅游区，在国内外享有盛名，被联合国评为“全球生态500佳村庄”“世界十佳自然村”。

Tengtou Village: China's premier ecological village. This national 5A-level tourist attraction stands out for its unique focus on ecological and comprehensive agriculture, and its green project that ensures clear waters and blue skies. Tengtou Village has developed into a distinctive ecological tourism area with international fame, earning accolades from the United Nations among "Global Ecological Habitats 500" and "World's Top Ten Harmonious Villages".

横坎头村——浙东红村。全国乡村治理示范村。村内红色资源丰富，以党建为引领发展红色文旅，依托“红绿结合”，走出了一条“红色引领绿色发展”的共富路。

---

① 资料来源：宁波市文化广电旅游局。
Source: Ningbo Municipal Bureau of Culture, Radio, Television and Tourism.

滕头村 Tengtou Village

Hengkantou Village: "Red Village" in East Zhejiang. The village serves as a national model for rural governance. Rich in revolutionary heritage, it has pioneered the development of red-themed cultural tourism under the guidance of the Communist Party of China. Its effective integration of historical (red) and ecological (green) resources has embarked on a prosperous path towards common prosperity.

韩岭村——浙东第一古村。位于东钱湖南岸，山水风情、文化韵味及民俗风情，成就了它独特的美，被誉为“中国梵高”的沙耆曾在韩岭村居住并留下了一批油画作品。现在的韩岭村以文艺格调丰满古村肌理，集聚各类文化艺术元素及活动，完成了古韵新生的蜕变。

Hanling Village: No.1 ancient village in East Zhejiang. Situated on the south shore of Dongqian Lake, the village showcases its charm with breathtaking landscape, cultural appeal and folk customs. Sha Qi, known as "Chinese Van Gogh",

横坎头村　Hengkantou Village

created a number of oil paintings when he lived here. Currently agglomerating diverse cultural and artistic elements and activities, the ancient village endowed with an artistic tinge becomes more attractive.

走马塘村——中国进士第一村。有“四明古郡，文献之邦，江山之胜，水陆之饶”之美誉，历朝历代出过76位进士，是上海世博会期间向全球推广的18个首批中国“魅力小城”之一。

韩岭村 Hanling Village

Zoumatang Village: China's Top Scholar Village. The ancient village in Yinzhou District holds the title of being one of Ningbo's oldest settlements, a place that witnessed the birth of numerous great scholars. Nestled amidst magnificent rivers and hills, this village exudes a captivating charm, embraced by fertile lands and flowing rivers.

走马塘村　Zoumatang Village

周末休闲游　Rural Tourism on Weekends

第1天 Day 1

四明山国家森林公园 Siming Mountains National Forest Park ●---● 横坎头村（入住民宿）Hengkantou Village (check in B&B)

第2天 Day 2

丹山赤水风景名胜区 Dan-Shan-Chi-Shui Scenic Area ●---● 四明山杖锡风景区 Zhangxi Scenic Area, Siming Mountains

三天微度假 Three-day Micro Vacation

第1天 Day 1

象山影视城 ●---● 松兰山旅游度假区（入住酒店、体验滨海运动）

Xiangshan Global Studios ●---● Ningbo Songlanshan Tourist Resort (check in hotel; enjoy beach sports)

第2天 Day 2

中国渔村 ●---● 石浦渔港古城 ●---● 沙塘湾村（入住民宿、品尝宁波小海鲜）

China Fishing Village ●---● Shipu Fishing Port Ancient Town ●---● Shatangwan Village(check-in B&B; savor local seafood)

第3天 Day 3

花岙岛 ●---● 中国水产城（购买海鲜）

Hua'ao Island ●---● China's Aquatic Products Capital (buy seafood)

玩转黄金周 Golden Week's Tour Routes

第1天 Day 1

宁波博物馆 ●---● 天一阁博物馆 ●---● 宁波帮博物馆 ●---● 中国港口博物馆

Ningbo Museum ●---● Tianyige Library Museum ●---● Ningbobang Museum ●---● China Port Museum

第2天 Day 2

宁波美术馆 ●---● 华茂美术馆 ●---● 韩岭美术馆 ●---● 韩岭艺文小镇

Ningbo Museum of Art ●---● Huamao Museum of Art Education ●---● Hanling Museum of Fine Arts ●---● Hanling town of Arts

第2—3天
Day 2–3

宁波方特·东方神话或东方欲晓 → 杭州湾国家湿地公园 → 鸣鹤古镇 → 上林湖青瓷文化传承园（入住民宿、品尝宁波道地农家菜）

Ningbo Fantawild Theme Park Oriental Heritage or Glorious Orient → Hangzhou Bay National Wetland Park → Minghe Ancient Town → Shanglin Lake Yue Kilns Site Park (check in B&B; try indigenous dishes)

第4—5天
Day 4–5

阳明古镇 → 河姆渡考古遗址公园 → 河姆渡遗址博物馆 → 慈城古县城（入住民宿、体验非遗文化、品尝道地小吃） → 保国寺、荪湖

Yangming Ancient Town → Hemudu Cultural Site → Hemudu Cultural Site Museum → Cicheng Ancient County (check in B&B; appreciate intangible heritage culture; taste local snacks) → Baoguo Temple, Sun Lake

第6—7天
Day 6–7

前童古镇 → 宁波森林温泉度假村 → 宁海湾（水上运动、休闲渔业）

Qiantong Ancient Town → Ninghai Forest Hot Spring Resort → Ninghai Bay (engage in water sports and recreational fisheries)

奔赴文化盛宴

Colorful Cultural Activities

宁波市城市展览馆　Ningbo City Exhibition Hall

宁波，2016年当选“东亚文化之都”，是国家历史文化名城。

Ningbo, selected as the "Culture Capital of East Asia" in 2016, is a national historical and cultural city.

在宁波，你可以全身心投入阅读，领略它的书香文化，可以享受高质而又全面的公共文化服务，可以感受极具特色又开放先进的浙东文化。

In Ningbo, you can immerse yourself in reading and appreciate its rich literary culture. You will have access to high-quality and distinctive public cultural services, and experience the unique, open, and proactive culture of east Zhejiang.

（一）博物致知
Museums

读懂一座城市，先从博物馆开始。宁波拥有80家博物馆[②]，它们如一颗颗璀璨明珠镶嵌在这座城市的文化之中，记录和展现着宁波这座城市从无到有的历史片段与文化符号，展现着地域文化经过历史风雨洗礼后留下来的不熄薪火。

Museums can be stepping stones for acquiring in-depth knowledge of a city. Ningbo is home to 80 museums, ranking eighth across China[②]. Like dazzling pearls embedded in the city's cultural fabric, these museums showcase the historical episodes and cultural symbols of Ningbo. They also display the enduring cultural heritage that has withstood the test of time and history.

宁波博物馆。国家一级博物馆，以展示宁波人文历史和艺术为主、具有地域特色的综合性博物馆，由首位中国籍“普利兹克建筑奖”得主王澍教授设计。博物馆的展品囊括了从史前河姆渡文化时期至近现代的珍贵青铜器、瓷器、竹刻、玉器、书画、金银器、民俗器具等。

Ningbo Museum. This national first-level comprehensive museum mainly specializes in humanities, history, and arts of Ningbo, bearing distinct regional characteristics. It is designed by Professor Wang Shu, the first Chinese recipient of the prestigious Pritzker Architecture Prize in 2012. As the youngest national first-

② 资料来源：宁波市文化广电旅游局，截至2023年8月。
Source: Ningbo Municipal Bureau of Culture, Radio, Television and Tourism, as of August 2023.

level museum in China, it boasts a collection of over 60000 artifacts, ranging from the prehistoric Hemudu culture to modern times. Its exhibits include bonze wares, ceramic wares, bamboo-carving objects, jade pieces, calligraphy and paintings, gold and silver wares, folk art, etc.

“宁波博物馆”微信公众号
WeChat Official Account of "Ningbo Museum"

宁波博物馆 Ningbo Museum

中国港口博物馆。国家一级博物馆，以港口文化为主题，我国规模最大、等级最高的大型港口专题博物馆，是挖掘港口历史、传承港口文化、传播海洋文明的重要基地，也是新世纪海上丝绸之路的重要文化支点。

China Port Museum. This is a national first-level museum and the premier destination for port enthusiasts. As the largest and most comprehensive museum dedicated to ports, it serves as a vital hub for exploring the rich history, cultural significance, and profound influence of ports. Additionally, it stands as a beacon of ocean civilization, representing the cultural core of the 21st century Maritime Silk Road.

“中国港口博物馆”微信公众号

WeChat Official Account of "China Port Museum"

中国港口博物馆 China Port Museum

宁波帮博物馆。国家二级博物馆，整体建筑呈现为“甬”字的形状，围合成“三江汇流”的场景意向。博物馆陈列由综合展区、专题展区和临时展览三部分组成，系统展示了明末至今宁波帮艰难困苦、玉汝于成的发展史诗。

Ningbobang Museum. The entire complex of this national second-level museum is designed to form the Chinese character "Yong", the name of the local Yong River and short for Ningbo. The layout of the building symbolizes the confluence of the Yuyao River, Fenghua River and Yong River. The museum is divided into three areas (comprehensive, thematic, and temporary exhibitions), systematically unfolding how Ningbo Native Merchants (*Ningbobang* in Chinese pinyin) forge ahead and make their dreams come true.

宁波帮博物馆　Ningbobang Museum

"宁波帮博物馆"微信公众号

WeChat Official Account of "Ningbobang Museum"

河姆渡遗址博物馆。包括遗址陈列馆和遗址考古现场馆，再现"干栏式"建筑及室内外先民生产、生活场景，获评"全国优秀爱国主义教育基地""全国百家爱国主义教育示范基地"。

Hemudu Cultural Site Museum. The museum inclueds two major parts: an exhibition hall (3200 m^2) and archaeological site hall (23000 m^2). The museum reproduces the stilted building and out-door and in-door production and living scenes of Chinese ancestors. It has been honored with the titles of "National Excellent Patriotism Education Base" and "Top 100 Patriotism Education Demonstration Base".

河姆渡遗址博物馆 Hemudu Cultural Site Museum

“河姆渡遗址博物馆”微信公众号
WeChat Official Account of "Hemudu Cultural Site Museum"

（二）书香氤氲
Libraries and Bookstores

从 24 小时城市书房，到 300 余个有声读书驿站，从校园里的经典诵读，到遍地开花的社区读书，宁波通过建设图书馆、布局城市书房（农家书屋）、开展阅读活动、推广数字阅读等方式，打造立体城市阅读格局，满足读者不同的阅读需求，全力建设“书香之城”。

A multi-dimensional urban reading pattern has been fostered in Ningbo through establishing libraries, laying out city's studies (and rural book houses), organizing reading activities, and promoting digital reading. This initiative of creating "City of Books" includes 24-hour city's studies, over 300 audio book stations, classic recitations on campuses, and widespread community reading events. These efforts aim to satisfy the diverse reading needs and experiences of readers.

宁波图书馆新馆。开设自助图书馆、创客空间、天一音乐馆、乔石书房等特色功能区域，创新推出流动图书馆、24 小时自助图书馆、网络图书馆、微信图书馆等便民惠民新服务模式，打造了“天一讲堂”等阅读推广特色品牌。截至 2023 年，图书馆馆藏量约 388 万册[③]。

Ningbo New Library. The new public library is well equipped with such popular library functions as self-service libraries, makerspace, Tianyi Music Hall, and Qiao Shi Study. And innovative services are fostered to benefit residents, including mobile libraries, bookmobiles, 24-hour self-service libraries, network libraries, WeChat libraries, mobile digital libraries. Moreover, the calling card – "Tianyi Lecture Hall" – helps to promote reading across the city. As of 2023, the library held a collection of 3.88 million volumes[③].

③ 资料来源：宁波市图书馆。
Source: Ningbo Library.

宁波图书馆新馆
Ningbo New Library

"宁波图书馆新馆"微信公众号
WeChat Official Account of "Ningbo New Library"

（三）视听盛宴
Art and Theaters

艺术是一种审美体验，而宁波就是这样一座"美"的城市。它美在设计，每一座艺术馆的建筑本身就是一件艺术品；它美在展品，每一件展品都藏着一个优美故事等待您的聆听；它美在音符，每一个音符都唱出了"音乐之城"的无限魅力。

Ningbo offers both visual feasts and auditory carnivals. The magnificent architecture of each art museum is an artwork itself; absorbing stories behind each exhibit are waiting for you to explore; this glamorous "City of Music" never fails to make newcomers linger on.

宁波美术馆。现有老外滩本部和东钱湖馆区。本部是"普利兹克建筑奖"获得者王澍的代表作品之一。馆内现有莫奈、塞尚、李可染、潘天寿、黄永玉、靳尚谊、全山石等国内外名家各类藏品，藏品数量居全国公立美术馆前列。

Ningbo Museum of Art. Currently, the museum is divided into two branches, the Old Bund Main Branch in Jiangbei District and the Dongqian Lake Branch in Yinzhou District. It holds more than 5600 pieces (sets) of domestic and foreign masterpieces from Claude Monet, Paul Cézanne, Li Keran, Pan Tianshou, Huang Yongyu, Jin Shangyi, Quan Shanshi among others, ranking among the best in terms of the number of collections.

"宁波美术馆"微信小程序
WeChat Official Account of "Ningbo Museum of Art"

宁波美术馆　Ningbo Museum of Art

宁波大剧院。位于姚江湾头“三江文化长廊”顶端，临江而建、三面环水。大剧院以自然声源为主。在此曾举办第九届中国戏剧节、第十五届亚洲艺术节等重大活动。

Ningbo Grand Theatre. The theater is situated at the top end of "Three Rivers Cultural Corridor" at the bayhead of the Yuyao River. It stands facing the river and surrounded by water on three sides. Its presentation of raw sound on the stage is adopted without using electroacoustic aid. The theatre plays host to many significant events such as the 9th Chinese Theatre Festival (2018) and the 15th Asian Arts Festival (2017).

“宁波大剧院”微信公众号
WeChat Official Account of "Ningbo Grand Theatre"

宁波大剧院 Ningbo Grand Theatre

宁波文化广场大剧院。一座能满足舞剧、歌剧、话剧、音乐会、综艺演出、会议等使用要求的多功能现代化剧场。《天鹅湖》《只此青绿》等一系列观众心目中的经典之作都曾在此演出。

Ningbo Cultural Plaza Grand Theatre. This multi-functional modern theater sets a stage for dance dramas, operas, dramas, concerts, variety shows and meetings. A series of classic performances including the Russian ballet *Swan Lake* and *The Journey of a Legendary Landscape Painting* (aka. *Only Blue and Green*) have drawn large audiences into the theater.

“宁波文化广场大剧院”微信公众号
WeChat Official Account of "Ningbo Cultural Plaza Grand Theatre"

宁波文化广场大剧院 Ningbo Cultural Plaza Grand Theatre

宁波音乐厅　Ningbo Concert Hall

宁波音乐厅。圆锥形的音乐殿堂像一颗晶莹剔透的明珠镶嵌在灵桥和琴桥之间，中央音乐学院等中国著名音乐院校的师生，中国电影乐团等著名专业团队，法国、德国、俄罗斯等国的交响乐团曾先后应邀来宁波音乐厅演出。

Ningbo Concert Hall. The conical hall, like a sparkling pearl, nestles between Ling bridge and Qin bridge. It sets a stage for a number of marvellous music performances. The invited superb performers include students and professors from renowned Chinese conservatoires like Central Conservatoire of Music, elite professional teams such as China Film Symphony Orchestra and foreign symphony orchestras from France, Germany, and Russia, etc.

（四）传世非遗
Intangible Cultural Heritage

宁波非物质文化遗产非常丰富，通过“三位一体”[非遗项目、项目传承人、传承（传播）基地三联合］非遗保护的宁波模式，甬剧等众多非遗项目或走出国门展示风采、或进入校园培育传人、或登上舞台成为精品……

Ningbo boasts a rich intangible cultural heritage. Its trinity model of heritage protection [integrating heritage projects and inheritors with inheritance (and dissemination) bases] has successfully showcased numerous heritage projects, such as Ningbo Yong opera and so on. These projects have either gained international exposure, entered educational programs to cultivate young practitioners, or undergone transformation into stage masterpieces.

甬剧。国家级非物质文化遗产，是以宁波方言演唱的地方戏曲剧种，适于演清装戏、三十年代西装旗袍戏和现代戏，紧跟时代，贴近现实生活，如传统戏《半把剪刀》《天要落雨娘要嫁》，现代戏《王鲲》《亮眼哥》等，受到广大观众的欢迎。

Ningbo Yong Opera. This national intangible cultural heritage is a local opera genre performed in the Ningbo dialect. The opera is suitable for actors and actresses to wear clothing pevalent in the Qing Dynasty, suits and cheongsam in the 1930s, and well-placed for contemporary plays in particular. Keeping pace with the times and closely related to real life, Yong Opera includes traditional plays like *Half Scissors* (*Banba Jiandao* in Chinese pinyin) and *Widow to Marry Rain to Fall* (*Tianyaoluoyu Niangyaojia* in Chinese pinyin), as well as modern plays like *Wang Kun* and *Bright-Eyed Brother* (*Liangyange* in Chinese pinyin), all of which have been warmly received by a wide audience.

越窑青瓷烧制技艺。国家级非物质文化遗产。越窑是中国古代最著名的青瓷窑系，其主要产地就是宁波慈溪上林湖一带，古代通过海上丝绸之路销往全球，对促进中外交流发挥过重要作用。目前，上林湖区域已形成集越窑青瓷传承、展示、科研、生产、销售等于一体的产业群。

The Yue Kiln Celadon Firing Technique. It is recognized as a national intangible cultural heritage in China. The Yue Kiln, one of the most famous ancient Chinese celadon kiln systems, primarily operated in the Shanglin Lake area of Cixi, Ningbo. In ancient times, its products were exported globally via the Maritime Silk

Road, playing a significant role in promoting international exchanges. Today, the Shanglin Lake region has developed into an industrial cluster that encompasses the inheritance, display, research, production, and sales of Yue Kiln celadon.

朱金漆木雕。国家级非物质文化遗产，是宁波市民间传统美术工艺，明清以来，朱金漆木雕广泛应用于民间日常生活，拥有著名的十里红妆、千工床、万工轿、万工船等堪称绝妙的民间工艺精品。位于宁波市鄞州区的朱金漆木雕艺术馆可供参观。

Ningbo Cinnabar and Gold Lacquer Woodcarving. This national intangible cultural heritage is a traditional folk art of Ningbo. Since the Ming and Qing dynasties, it has been widely used in daily life, with famous examples including dowry, wooden beds, bridal sedan chairs, and wooden boats, all considered exquisite folk craftsmanship. The Ningbo Cinnabar and Gold Lacquer Art Museum, located in Yinzhou District, is open to visitors.

董氏儿科医术。国家级非物质文化遗产，是中国海派中医儿科的主要流派，至今已有200多年历史，门生遍及全国，医术蜚声海内外。第四代传人董廷瑶先生被誉为当代中医儿科泰斗。

Dong's Pediatric Medicine. This main school of TCM pediatrics, listed as a national intangible cultural heritage, boasts a history of more than two hundred years. Its trained disciples are spread across China, enjoying a high reputation at home and abroad. Mr. Dong Tingyao, the fourth-generation heir of the school, is acclaimed as the leading pediatrician in contemporary TCM pediatrics.

（五）节庆会展
Festivals and Exhibitions

宁波节庆会展活动种类繁多，既有展现宁波历史文化的传统节庆，也有与国际接轨、国际文化交流前沿的国际性展会。通过传统节庆活动，您可以深刻体验宁波地道的民俗文化；通过国际性会展活动，您可以领略全球各地的民俗风情。

Diversified festivals and exhibitions in Ningbo range from traditional festivals showing local history and culture to international exhibitions promoting international cultural exchanges. You can savor Ningbo's folk culture at traditional festivals, and meanwhile enjoy global folk customs when attending international expositions.

中国（象山）开渔节。于每年9月中旬举办，是以感恩海洋、保护海洋为主题、以渔文化为主线的海洋民俗文化类节庆，已经成为宁波市三大主要节庆之一，并跻身国家文旅部十大民俗节庆活动行列。

China Fishing Season Festival in Xiangshan. Held on mid-September every year, it worships the seas and celebrates the local marine folk culture. The festival has become one of the three major festivals in Ningbo and has been recognized as one of the top ten folk festival events by the National Tourism Administration.

中国（象山）开渔节 China Fishing Season Festival

中国徐霞客开游节。以明代杰出地理学家、旅行家、文学家徐霞客命名，于每年5月19日（中国旅游日）举办。是集民俗文艺表演、体育竞技、招商引资、经贸洽谈、商品展销和旅游休闲于一体的大型文化旅游节庆活动。

China Xu Xiake Tourism Festival. This festival is named after Xu Xiake (1587-1641), a famous Chinese geographer, traveler, and travel writer of the Ming Dynasty (1368-1644). Held on May 19th (The China Tourism Day) every year, it features with a variety of activities, including folklore and cultural performances, sports competitions, investment promotion, trade and economic negotiations, commodity exhibitions and sales, and tourism and leisure.

中国徐霞客开游节 China Xu Xiake Tourism International Festival

中国－中东欧国家博览会暨国际消费品博览会。我国面向中东欧国家的唯一国家级展会。博览会涵盖产业投资、商品交易、科技互动、人文艺术交流等多个主题活动内容。

China-Central and Eastern European Countries (CEEC) Expo and International Consumer Goods Fair. This is China's only state-level exhibition targeted at CEEC. The expo covers a wide range of activities, such as industrial investment, commodity trading, scientific and technological exchanges, and humanistic and artistic exchanges.

海丝之路文化和旅游博览会。每年举办一届，每届有数十个国家和地区以及国内近百座城市展商参展。2023 年，博览会围绕“弘扬丝路精神 共创美好生活”等主题，成为全城联动、全民共享的文化盛宴。

Maritime Silk Road Culture and Tourism Expo. Exhibitors from dozens of countries and regions and nearly 100 cities of China participated in the Maritime Silk Road Culture and Tourism Expo every year. In 2023, under the theme of

中国一中东欧国家博览会　China-CEEC Expo

"Carrying forward the spirit of the Silk Road and creating a better future", it has become a "cultural feast" shared by the city and the whole nation.

浙江书展。宁波是浙江书展的永久举办地，每年举办一届。2023 年浙江书展围绕“阅读引领 精神共富”等主题，邀请知名作家和文化名家亲临主会场，组织开展茅奖作者对话、天一阁论坛等重要活动，以及新书分享会等阅读推广活动，是促进全民精神共富的重要文化平台。

Zhejiang Book Fair. This is an annual fair permanently held in Ningbo. Under "Reading Leads to Spiritual Enrichment" and other themes, the fair has been attended by renowned writers and cultural figures. Its main activities include the dialogue between Mao Dun Literature Prize winners as well as the Tianyi Pavilion Forum, and reading promotion activities such as new book releases are organized alongside. This fair is currently recognized as a crucial cultural platform for showcasing Zhejiang's major cultural labels and fostering a collective spiritual wealth among the populace.

2023 年海丝之路文化和旅游博览会　2023 Maritime Silk Road Culture and Tourism Expo

2023 年浙江书展　2023 Zhejiang Book Fair

舌尖上的宁波
A Bite of Ningbo

宁波美食　Ningbo cuisine

一方水土一方产物，宁波位于东海之滨，山林茂密，气候温和，山珍海味极为丰富。甘甜蔬果、新鲜海产、特色小吃，还有楼茂记、升阳泰、缸鸭狗等中华老字号品牌，在宁波，你不仅可以吃到人间美味，更能体验一种全新的文化。来到宁波，一定要尝一尝最正宗的宁波味道。

Ningbo dwells by the coast of the East China Sea, with lush forests, mild climate, and local delicacies. Savoring fruits, vegetables, seafood and local snacks can provide a way for you to experience a new culture. During your visit to Ningbo, we highly recommend indulging in the authentic local delicacies that epitomize the gastronomic culture of this vibrant port city.

（一）蔬果海鲜
Fruits, Vegetables and Seafood

宁波物产丰富，在苍茫的山林溪间，盛产桃李、杨梅、柑橘等水果；在漫长的近海及岸边，鱼虾蟹贝更是常年不绝。

Ningbo abounds in mountains (hills), rivers (streams), as well as coasts, and thus local produces. In particular, peaches, waxberries, and tangerines are among the exemplars of its native fruits and vegetables; fish, shrimps, crabs, and shellfish are always available.

杨梅。苏东坡有言，“闽广荔枝、西凉葡萄，未若吴越杨梅”。宁波杨梅有大乌杨梅、白杨梅及红种、粉红种等品类，其中当数慈溪和余姚的最负盛名。杨梅可生吃或泡杨梅酒、煮糖水杨梅、做杨梅饮料或杨梅干。

杨梅 Waxberry

Waxberry. "Waxberries in Zhejiang and Jiangsu belittle litchis in Fujian and Guangdong as well as grapes in Xinjiang," said Su Dongpo, China's poet in Northern Song Dynasty. Ningbo waxberry includes white waxberry, red waxberry and pink waxberry, among which waxberry in Cixi and Yuyao are the most famous. The fruit can be eaten fresh or made into infused waxberry wine, boiled but sweetened waxberries, waxberry juice, and dried waxberries.

奉化水蜜桃。奉化栽桃史已有2000多年，奉化水蜜桃是中国四大传统名桃之一，是中国国家地理标志产品，有"琼浆玉露，瑶池珍品"之美誉。

Fenghua Honey Peach. With a rich history of over 2000 years and renowned across China, Fenghua honey peach is listed as one of national geographical indications (GI) products.

奉化水蜜桃 Fenghua Honey Peach

象山红美人。象山自古产橘，宋朝便以金橘入贡，有"中国柑橘之乡"的美称。尤其是"象山红美人"，拥有柑、橘、橙三种血统，被誉为柑橘界的"爱马仕"。

Xiangshan Tangerines. Xiangshan has been growing tangerines since ancient times, and in the Song Dynasty, tangerines were chosen as tribute to the royal family. Hongmeiren, to be specific, blends the taste of citrus, tangerine and orange and is nowadays known as the "Hermès" of citrus.

象山红美人 Xiangshan Tangerines

宁海白枇杷。白枇杷是宁海县的特色农产品之一，具有淡黄偏白的果皮、乳白

宁海白枇杷　White Loquat in Ninghai

色的果肉，被称为“宁海白”，品质超过国内外同类产品。

White Loquat in Ninghai. This white loquat, featuring light yellow skin and milky white pulp, is one representative agricultural product of Ninghai County. It is commonly called "Ninghai White", topping similar products at home and abroad.

奉化芋艿头　Fenghua Taro

奉化芋艿头。奉化广植芋艿头已有700多年的历史，以前葛产的芋艿头最负盛名。芋艿头可烘蒸、生烤、热炒、白切、做糊、浇汤。

Fenghua Taro. The planting of taro in Fenghua can be dated back to over 700 years ago. And the taro from Qiange village is the most famous one.Taro can be cooked in various ways, i.e., steaming, roasting, frying, slicing, etc.

梭子蟹。野生梭子蟹是宁波传统的冬令珍馐。蟹黄色味俱佳，食之别有风味，居海鲜之首。

Swimming Crab. Wild swimming crab is a traditional winter delicacy in Ningbo. The rich flavor and unique taste of crab roe make it a standout among seafood.

长街蛏子。“西施舌”是长街蛏子的别称。长街蛏子已成功注册国家地理标志证明商标。

Changjie Razor Clam. Changjie town of Ninghai County is known as the "home of razor clams" in China, and Changjie razor clam has been successfully registered as a National GI Trademark.

奉化蚶子。奉化蚶子因无“含口泥”而著称，冠名“奉蚶”，是蚶子中较著名的一种。早在唐朝奉蚶就被列为贡品。

Fenghua Ark Clam. The Fenghua ark clam is a particularly famous variety, known for being free of "mouth grit" and earning the name "Feng clam." It was chosen as tribute to the royal family since the late Tang Dynasty.

梭子蟹 Swimming Crab

长街蛏子 Razor Clam

奉化蚶子 Fenghua Ark Clam

（二）传统佳肴
Traditional Cuisine

宁波人饮食以海鲜为主，宁波菜简称“甬菜”，以咸、鲜、臭闻名，是浙菜中非常具有特色的一个品种。宁波菜以烹制山珍海味著称，尤以蒸、烤、烧、炸、炒各类鱼鲜见长。

Ningbo cuisine, often referred to as "Yong cuisine," is renowned for its emphasis on seafood. Its savory, fresh, and distinctively pungent flavors make it a unique aspect of Zhejiang cuisine. Its preparation of mountain delicacies and seafood particularly excels in steamed, roasted, braised, fried, and stir-fried fish dishes.

红膏炝蟹。“红膏炝蟹咸咪咪，大汤黄鱼摆咸齑”，红膏炝蟹号称“宁波第一冷盘”，临近过年正是红膏炝蟹最盛行之时。

Red Cream Salted Crab. "The salted crab with roe, salty and savory, and the yellow croaker soup presented with salted vegetables are renowned local delicacies." In particular, salted crab with roe is an acclaimed cold dish in Ningbo. New Year and Spring Festival (the Chinese New Year) are generally the peak season for locals to eat salted crab.

红膏炝蟹　Red Cream Salted Crab

醉泥螺。黄泥螺状如蚕豆，壳薄如纸，以产于慈溪龙山一带的为佳。醉泥螺有黄酒香气，是宁波常见的海鲜冷菜。

Pickled Mud Snail. The mud snail cultured in Longshan town, Cixi is considered as the best. The pickled mud snail embracing the aroma of yellow rice wine is a well-known cold dish in Ningbo.

冰糖甲鱼。宁波传统名菜之一，又称“独占鳌头”，具有滋补养生的功效。

Crystal Sugar Turtle. This famous traditional dish in Ningbo is also known as "Number One Scholar Turtle", boasting rich nutrition and health-boosting properties.

醉泥螺 Pickled Mud Snail

雪菜大黄鱼。大黄鱼寓意黄金万两、年年有余。本菜品以大黄鱼和本地产的雪里蕻咸齑为主要原料，具有鱼嫩、菜香、汤鲜的特点。

Yellow Croaker with Pickled Potherb Mustard. Yellow croaker symbolizes abundant wealth and prosperity. This dish primarily features yellow croaker and locally sourced pickled vegetables as its main ingredients, known for its tender fish, aromatic vegetables, and savory broth.

冰糖甲鱼 Crystal Sugar Turtle

宁式鳝糊。宁波人宴席上的压轴菜，寓意“善始善终”，具有鲜香嫩滑、油润肥美的特色。

Ningbo-Style Braised River Eel. This local dish cannot be missed at a banquet, which means "a good beginning will end well." It is valued for its fresh, fragrant, tender, and smooth texture with a rich and luscious taste.

雪菜大黄鱼　Yellow Croaker with Pickled Potherb Mustard

奉化油焖笋。浓稠的酱汁充分包裹住每一块笋，每嚼一口，爽脆而不老，酥嫩而不烂。可直接吃或下酒、拌饭、煮面、炒菜。

Fenghua Oil-Braised Bamboo Shoots. The thick sauce fully coats every bamboo shoot segment, offering a bite that is crunchy yet not hard, and tender without falling apart. It can be eaten directly, fried with vegetables, mixed with rice, cooked with noodles, or stir-fried with vegetables. It is also a good choice while drinking.

宁式鳝糊　Ningbo-Style Braised River Eel

奉化油焖笋　Fenghua Oil-Braised Bamboo Shoots

（三）特色小吃
Signature Snacks

宁波小吃最主要的特征是以米制品为主，广泛采用苔菜、艾青叶等本地土特产作为配料，风味独特、做工精细，可与“苏式”“广式”糕点等相媲美。

Ningbo snacks are characterized by their primary use of rice-based products, extensively incorporating local specialties such as moss cabbage and mugwort leaves as ingredients. These snacks are unique in flavor and meticulously crafted, rivaling the delicacies of Suzhou-style and Cantonese-style pastries.

宁波汤圆。汤圆是中国传统小吃之一，象征着家人团圆、生活圆满幸福。每逢佳节，宁波人都会吃碗汤圆以寄托思乡之情。

Ningbo Tangyuan (aka. Ningbo Rice Dumplings). Tangyuan, is a traditional Chinese snack. It is a symbol of family reunion and happiness. During festive occasions, eating a bowl of sweet Tangyuan conveys bouts of homesickness.

宁波麻糍。谐音“呒事”，寓意平安无事，是宁波清明祭祀的主祭品，多是掺着艾青的青麻糍。

Ningbo Maci. The Chinese pronunciation of Maci in Ningbo dialect is similar to "wu shi" (meaning "no worries"), symbolizing peace and safety. The Maci, often mixed with mugwort to create green rice cakes, is the main offering of the Qingming Festival rituals in Ningbo.

宁波汤圆 Ningbo Tangyuan

宁波麻糍 Ningbo Maci

慈城年糕。年糕寓意“年年高”，可以做成咸齑年糕汤、白蟹炒年糕、烤菜年糕等多款菜肴。慈城水磨年糕手工制作技艺入选浙江省非物质文化遗产代表性项目名录。

Cicheng Rice Cake (Nian Gao). The Chinese pronunciation for the rice cake is similar to that of "Happy New Year". The rice cake can be boiled in soup, dotted with sweet-scented osmanthus, fried with crabs or roasted with vegetables. The handicraft of making Cicheng rice cakes has been included in the representative project list of intangible cultural heritage of Zhejiang Province.

慈城年糕 Cicheng Rice Cake

溪口千层饼。在奉化溪口已经有100多年历史，外形四方，内分27层，层次分明，金黄透绿，香酥松脆，甜中带咸。

Xikou Qianceng Cookies. The history of this traditional snack extends about 100 years. The cookies, crisp, sweet, and a bit salty, is square with 27 layers of golden color tinted with green.

溪口千层饼　Xikou Qianceng Cookies

梁弄大糕。用大米磨粉制作，填入豆沙馅再蒸熟，雪白的大糕上通常印有“恭喜发财”“吉祥如意”等祝福语。

Liangnong Rice Cake. Prior to steaming, it is first made from ground rice and filled with sweet red bean paste. This as-processed white cake is often imprinted with blessings such as "Wishing You Prospcrity and Wealth" and "Good Luck."

梁弄大糕　Liangnong Rice Cake

点燃运动激情

Sports and Fun

五一广场 Wuyi Plaza

宁波是一座时尚城市、一座运动城市。在2021年东京奥运会上，宁波健儿勇夺五枚金牌，此后宁波被中国奥委会授予“奥运冠军之城”称号，“运动宁波”的城市品牌不断“出圈”。

Ningbo is a trendy and dynamic city. Athletes from this coastal city have won five gold medals at Tokyo Olympic Games in 2021, and then Ningbo was awarded the commemorative "City of Olympic Champions" trophy by the Chinese Olympic Committee in 2022. The city brand of "Sports Ningbo" has been gaining widespread recognition.

在城市社区，“十分钟健身圈”可以满足你日常健身需求；在山水间，时尚流行的运动项目可以供你周末休闲；在业余时间里，每年丰富的赛事和40余家体育单项协会等待你的参与。

In its urban communities, the "10-minute fitness circles" can meet your daily fitness needs; and amidst its rural areas, modish sports activities are available for your weekend leisure. In your spare time, a wealth of annual sporting events and over 40 sports associations await your participation.

（一）健身场馆
Sports Venues

作为国家体育消费试点城市，宁波始终致力于打造群众身边的体育服务生态圈，已经形成包含全民健身中心、综合体育馆、多功能运动场、体育公园、百姓健身房等健身场所的城市社区“十分钟健身圈”和全市“十五分钟健身圈”，可以全季、全时、全龄满足市民健身需求。

As a national pilot city for sports consumption, Ningbo has always been committed to building a sports service ecosystem around the masses. A "ten-minute fitness circle" of urban communities and a "fifteen-minute fitness circle" of the whole city have been established, including national fitness centers, comprehensive gymnasiums, multi-functional stadiums, sports parks, and people's gymnasiums. They can meet the fitness needs of the public in all seasons, at all times and for all ages.

宁波市体育中心。由富邦体育场、雅戈尔体育馆、网球馆、训练馆、训练场、高尔夫球练习场、游泳健身中心及附属设施等组成，是宁波市最早的市级体育健身场所。曾先后成功承办中国体育大会、亚俱杯东亚足球四强赛、中国羽毛球超级赛、中国男子篮球职业联赛（CBA）八一队主场赛事、中国足球甲B联赛等重大体育赛事。

Ningbo Sports Center. The center consists of Fubang Stadium, Youngor Gymnasium, Tennis Stadium, Training Hall, Training Ground, Golf Driving Range, Swimming and Fitness Center and affiliated facilities. It has successfully hosted major sports events such as the National Sports Festival of China, the EAFF East Asian Cup Quarterfinals, the China Badminton Super League (CBSL), Bayi home games of the CBA Basketball League, and the China Football Association Super League B.

宁波市体育中心　Ningbo Sports Center

宁波奥体中心。包括“一场三馆一中心”，即体育场、体育馆、游泳馆、综合训练馆（全民健身馆）、国际体育交流中心，是宁波市最大的体育馆，具备承接国家级赛事和综合训练的基本功能，且能够满足全民健身、运动休闲、文体活动的需求。

Ningbo Olympic Sports Center. The center comprises a stadium, an indoor sports arena, a swimming hall, a comprehensive training hall (also serving as a fitness center for the public), and an international sports exchange center. It is the largest sports complex in Ningbo, equipped with the essential facilities to host national-level competitions and comprehensive training. Additionally, it can meet the public's needs for fitness, sports recreation, and cultural activities.

宁波奥体中心　Ningbo Olympic Sports Center

宁波市全民健身指导中心。包含壁球、乒乓球、击剑、羽毛球、网球、门球、舞蹈等多种运动项目的健身场所，是一个集健身、比赛、培训、娱乐、休闲、社交于一体的综合性体育场所。

Ningbo Public Fitness Instruction Center. This sports complex encompasses services in fitness, competitions, training, entertainment, leisure, and socializing. It offers a variety of fitness facilities for squash, table tennis, fencing, badminton, tennis, gateball, dance, and more.

宁波市全民健身指导中心　Ningbo Public Fitness Instruction Center

宁波市滨江体育公园。包含塑胶跑道和自行车道，以及篮球场、气排球场、笼式足球场、门球场、地掷球场和儿童嬉水广场。

Ningbo's Riverside Sports Park. The park features a variety of facilities including a synthetic track and bike path, basketball courts, air volleyball courts, enclosed soccer fields, gateball courts, petanque courts, and an outdoor water play area for kids.

鄞州惠风体育馆。经营管理鄞州网球、游泳中心和体育馆。其中鄞州体育馆可容纳4500位观众，包括篮球馆、排球馆、羽毛球馆等场馆。宁波（鄞州）网球中心是一块能够举行国际性网球赛事的国际标准场地，可同时容纳近4000人观看比赛，连续12年成功承办ITF、ATP、WTA和CTA等国际国内高等级网球赛事。

Yinzhou Huifeng Sports Center. The center operates the tennis center and the swimming center of Yinzhou district, and Yinzhou Gymnasium. In particular, the gymnasium – capable of accommodating 4500 spectators – includes stadiums for basketball, volleyball, badminton, and more. Ningbo (Yinzhou) Tennis Center is an international standard venue capable of hosting international tennis tournaments, with seating for nearly 4000 spectators. For twelve consecutive years, fourteen high-level tennis events

宁波市滨江体育公园　Ningbo's Riverside Sports Park

鄞州惠风体育馆　Yinzhou Huifeng Sports Center

(international and domestic), including ITF, ATP, WTA, and CTA tournaments, have been successfully hosted here.

北仑体艺中心。由比赛馆和训练馆组成。自“中国女排主场”落户北仑以来，先后承办了国际排球赛事和篮球、乒乓球等项目的国内外重大比赛，被国家体育总局命名为“国家宁波北仑体育训练基地”，成为浙江省唯一获此殊荣的综合体育训练基地。

Beilun Sports and Arts Center. The center – composed of a competition hall and a training hall – is the home venue for the Chinese women's volleyball team. It has hosted numerous international volleyball competitions as well as major domestic and international events in basketball, table tennis, and other sports. The center is also designated by the General Administration of Sport of China as the "Ningbo Beilun National Sports Training Base", the only as-titled comprehensive sports training base in Zhejiang Province.

北仑体艺中心 Beilun Sports and Arts Center

（二）户外运动
Outdoor Sports

宁波具有“三江三湾大花园”的空间格局，江、河、湖、海、山的自然资源为宁波种下了运动基因。

Ningbo is a garden city embracing rivers and bays, in which its natural resources (i.e., rivers, lakes, seas and mountains) offer abundant venues for outdoor sports.

在宁波，你可以选择驾着帆船在东海上破浪，可以选择坐上龙舟在东钱湖里遨游，可以选择持着登山杖在四明山上前行，还可以选择骑上自行车在三江沿岸穿梭。

In this coastal city, you can choose to sail a sailboat to break the waves on the East China Sea, ride a dragon boat in Dongqian Lake, or go hiking on Siming Mountains. A bicycle ride along the water ways of the city will be another good choice.

浙江海洋运动中心（亚帆中心）。浙江省首个可承办水上运动国际 A 级比赛的场地。亚帆中心包括比赛训练中心、水上运动基地及港池等区域，可容纳 1000 个泊位，是杭州第 19 届亚运会帆船比赛场地。

Zhejiang Ocean Sports Center (Asian Sailing Center). Located in Songlan Mountain Scenic Spot of Xiangshan County, it is the first venue in Zhejiang Province that can host international A-level competitions of water sports. The Asian Sailing Center includes areas such as the competition training center, water sports base, harbor basin and other areas, with a capacity of 1000 berths. It is the sailing venue for the 19th Asian Games in Hangzhou.

宁海国家登山健身步道。包括 100 千米的登山步道和 50 千米的山地自行车道，登山步道以山间天然路径原生态为基础，是中国第一个符合国家标准的登山健身步道，也是国家登山运动训练基地，定期举办中国登山户外运动技能资质大赛、宁海越野挑战赛等赛事。

Ninghai National Hiking Trail. It includes 100 kilometers of hiking trails and 50 kilometers of mountain biking trails; the former – based on the original

浙江海洋运动中心 Zhejiang Ocean Sports Center

宁海国家登山健身步道 Ninghai National Hiking Trail

ecology of natural paths in the mountains – are the first hiking and fitness trail in China that meets the national standards. This trail is also approved as a national training base for mountaineering and regularly organizes events such as the China Mountaineering and Outdoor Sports Skills Qualification Competition and the Ninghai Rally Sports Challenge.

宁波国际赛车场　Ningbo International Speedway

宁波国际赛车场。拥有国际汽联FIA认证的二级赛道，可举办各类型房车、方程式、摩托车场地赛。在此已举办过WTCC世界房车锦标赛、国际汽联F4中国锦标赛、CFGP中国方程式大奖赛等大型赛事。

Ningbo Internat-ional Speedway. It is equipped with a FIA-certified Grade II track, capable of hosting all types of touring car, formula and motorcycle venue races. Among its hosted large-scale events are the WTCC World Touring Car Championship, the FIA F4 China Championship and the CFGP China Formula Grand Prix.

鄞江攀岩公园。利用上化山古采石场的岩壁资源，设有栈道式攀岩、自然岩攀岩和标准人工岩壁攀岩等项目场地，是“一带一路”国际攀岩大师赛等国际攀岩赛事的举办地。

Yinjiang Rock Climbing Park. Located in Yinjiang town of Haishu district, the park utilizes the rock wall resources of the ancient quarry of Shanghuashan Mountain, featuring projects such as trestle climbing, natural rock climbing and standard artificial rock wall climbing. It is the venue for international climbing events such as the "Belt and Road" International Climbing Masters Tournament.

宁波山地车越野公园。“天然氧吧＋体育赛事”场地，可以服务山地车、滑步车、越野跑、野外定向、休闲健步等众多项目。多条赛道可满足不同级别的车手需要。

Ningbo Mountain Bike Park. This venue of "Natural Oxygen Bar + Sports Events" is capable of serving such programs as mountain biking, scootering, trail running, orienteering, and recreational hiking. Multiple tracks are available to meet the needs of riders at different skill levels.

鄞江攀岩公园　Yinjiang Rock Climbing Park

宁波山地车越野公园　Ningbo Mountain Bike Park

宁波商量岗滑雪场。依托“四明第一山”得天独厚的气候与地理优势，集旅游观光、休闲度假、冰雪娱乐、健身养生于一体。场内设有简易滑雪、滑冰、滑圈、马拉雪橇、冰上芭蕾、雪上飞碟等冰雪娱乐项目。

Ningbo Shanglianggang Ski Resort. Thanks to the unique climate and geographic advantages of "Premier Mountain in Siming", it offers a comprehensive experience that includes tourism, leisure vacations, ice-snow entertainment, and health and fitness activities. The resort is equipped with basic skiing, ice skating, skating circles, horse-drawn sledding, ice ballet, snow flying saucer and other winter entertainment activities.

商量岗滑雪场 Shanglianggang Ski Resort

（三）赛事活动
Sporting Events

宁波的赛事活动非常丰富，曾举办过中日韩青少年运动会、亚洲举重锦标赛、龙舟世界杯、世界女排联赛、ILCA 亚洲锦标赛等国际高能级体育赛事。2023 年杭州亚运会帆船赛期间，WTA250 网球赛、奥运会女子排球资格赛等将全民健身的氛围推向高潮。未来，宁波还将引进和创办更多顶级赛事。

Ningbo has hosted a wealth of high-profile sporting events, including the 24th China-Japan-Korea Junior Sports Exchange Meet (2016), the 2019 Asian Weightlifting Championships, the 2019 ICF Dragon Boat World Cup, the FIVB Volleyball Women's Nations League (2019, 2021, 2023), and the ILCA Asian (Open) Sailing Championship 2023. During the sailing event of the 2023 Hangzhou Asian Games, the WTA 250 tennis tournament and Volleyball Women's Olympic Qualifying Tournament were also held in Ningbo, elevating the public's enthusiasm for fitness to a new climax. In the future, Ningbo will introduce and establish more top events.

WTA 宁波网球公开赛。WTA 组织（国际女子网球协会）2023 赛季在中国新设的一项硬地网球赛事。从 2023 年起，将连续十年在宁波举办。

WTA Ningbo Tennis Open. This newly introduced hard-court tournament by the Women's Tennis Association (WTA) was set to debut in the 2023 season in China. Scheduled to take place in Ningbo, it will run annually for a decade starting from 2023.

2024—2025 年亚洲羽毛球锦标赛。世界顶级、亚洲地区最高级别的羽毛球赛事。2024 年 1 月 23 日，中国羽毛球协会发布公告，确定宁波市为 2024—2025 年亚洲羽毛球锦标赛办赛城市。本次亚锦赛是亚洲地区羽毛球运动员争夺巴黎奥运会参赛资格的最后一站积分赛，意义非凡。

2024-2025 Badminton Asia Championships. The championships are the pinnacle of world-class badminton competition, representing the highest level of play in the Asian region. On January 23, 2023, the Chinese Badminton Association announced that Ningbo city has been selected as the host city for the upcoming 2024-2025 season of Badminton Asia Championships. This event is set to serve as the final qualifying event for badminton athletes in the Asian region to secure their spots at the 2024 Paris Olympic Games.

2023 年 WTA 宁波网球公开赛 2023 WTA Ningbo Tennis Open

宁波马拉松赛 Ningbo International Marathon

2026 年世界举重锦标赛。2028 年洛杉矶奥运会举重比赛的首场资格赛。在 2023 年 12 月举办的国际举重联合会执委会上，宁波正式获得 2026 年世界举重锦标赛举办权。这是世界举重锦标赛时隔 28 年再度落户中国。

The 2026 IWF World Weightlifting Championships. The championships will serve as the first qualifying event for the weightlifting competition at the 2028 Los Angeles Olympics. During the IWF Executive Board meeting held in December 2023, Ningbo was officially chosen to host the 2026 edition of the IWF World Championships. This marks the return of the event to China after 28 years.

宁波马拉松赛。2015 年首届办赛，2019 年赛事获得“中国田径铜牌赛事”称号。每届马拉松赛都将宁波的地标融入赛道设计，向世界传递扬帆逐海、勇立潮头的城市精神。

Ningbo International Marathon. The event was first organized in 2015, and four years later awarded the "China Athletics Association (CAA) Bronze Label Road Race". Each year's marathon incorporates Ningbo's landmarks into the course design, conveying to the world the city's spirit of sailing to the seas and standing at the forefront of the tide.

宁海越野挑战赛。赛事始于 2013 年，是国际超级越野跑巡回赛 UTWT 的其中一站，荣获 2021 年国家体育产业示范项目。

Ultra-Trail® Ninghai. The event started in 2013 and was confirmed as the latest race added to the Ultra-Trail World Tour (UTWT). It was honored as a national sports industry demonstration project in 2021.

中国 – 中东欧国际帆船赛。2023 年 5 月 20 日，首届中国 – 中东欧国际帆船赛在东钱湖举行。除中国和中东欧国家的参赛队伍、俱乐部队、企业代表队外，赛会还邀请了其他国家队伍参加。

China-Central and Eastern Europe International Regatta. On May 20, 2023, the first China-Central and Eastern Europe International Regatta opened at Dongqian Lake. In addition to teams from China and CEEC, club and corporate teams, and teams from other countries were invited to participate.

首届中国 – 中东欧国际帆船赛
1st China – Central and Eastern Europe International Regatta

“一带一路”国际跑酷大师赛。主赛为国际跑酷大师赛，设有个人技巧赛、个人竞速赛、障碍追逐赛和单项挑战赛（金刚定点）四个项目；附赛为少儿跑酷赛和街头健身表演赛，还设有小轮车攀爬、潮流集市等文艺活动。

"Belt and Road" International Parkour Masters. Its main event is the International Parkour Masters Tournament, featuring four contests: Individual Skill Race, Individual Speed Race, Obstacle Chase Race and Single Challenge Race (Vajra Fixation); the side events are the Children's Parkour Race and Street Fitness Performance Race. There are also cultural and artistic activities such as small-wheeled vehicle climbing and trendy bazaar.

健身服务查询与预约平台
Enquiry and Reservation Platform for Fitness Services

依托“浙里办”浙江省政务服务客户端，开辟“浙里健身”服务板块，围绕体育场地设施、体育赛事活动、科学健身指导等全民健身需求，建立高质量体育公共服务体系，构建十五分钟体育服务圈。

Leveraging "Zheliban" (Zhejiang's online government service platform), this enquiry and reservation platform opens up the application of "Zheli fitness" on sports facilities, sports events and activities, and scientific fitness guidance. It is hoped to establish a high-quality sports public service system and build a 15-minute sports service circle.

“浙里办”App　　“浙里办”支付宝小程序　　“浙里办”微信小程序

第一步：下载、打开“浙里办”，注册并登录；

Step 1: Download and open "Zheliban", register and login;

第二步：在首页搜索“浙里健身”，并点击进入；

Step 2: Search for "Zheli Fitness" on the homepage and click to enter;

第三步：“您当前位置”选择宁波或者您所需区域；

Step 3: Select Ningbo or your desired area for "Your current location";

第四步：点击选择您需要的体育场地、赛事活动、健身指导、体育组织等板块进行查询或预约。

Step 4: Click to select the sports venues, events and activities, fitness guidance, sports organizations, or other sections you need to inquire or book.

引爆消费热潮
Shopping Guide

宁波时尚创意中心（NFCC） Ningbo Fashion Creative Center

宁波自古以来就是繁荣的商业城市，遍地商铺、商贾云集，一直是中国的重要商业中心。2023年，宁波位列福布斯中国消费活力城市排行榜第12位。无论是时尚潮流的商业综合体、独具韵味的特色街区，还是热闹非凡的专业市场，在这座活力消费之城，总有一个地方能满足你的消费需求。

Ningbo has been a prosperous commercial city and an important business center nationwide since ancient times. This port city in east China ranked 12th on the 2023 Forbes China Consumer Vitality Cities List. There is always a place (e.g., a trendy commercial complex, a unique neighborhood, or a bustling professional market) to satisfy your consumption needs in this vibrant city.

（一）购物商城
Shopping Malls

目前，宁波已形成五大泛商圈，包括天一商圈、东部商圈、南部商圈、万象城商圈、奥莱商圈，年销售总额逾450亿元[④]。

At present, Ningbo has formed five major commercial zones, including Tianyi, Eastern, Southern, The Mixc and Shanjing Outlets. The total sales revenue of these five major commercial zones exceeded 45 billion yuan annually[④].

天一广场——目前国内最大的“一站式”购物商业广场。由22座欧陆风情浓郁的现代建筑群组成，集合了“吃、行、娱、购、游”五大要素，涵盖10个商业区，集中了300多家店铺，是宁波市中心最具活力、最时尚的商业广场。

Tianyi Square: The largest "one-stop" commercial complex in China. It consists of a cluster of 22 modern European-style buildings. Tianyi Square integrates five elements of "food, transportation, entertainment, shopping and tourism", covering 10 business districts and housing more than 300 stores. It is recognized as the most dynamic and fashionable commercial plaza in the center of Ningbo.

④ 资料来源：宁波市商务局。
Source: Ningbo Municipal Bureau of Commerce.

天一广场　Tianyi Square

和义大道——汇聚国际顶级品牌的高档购物中心。集聚了众多国际著名品牌和各类特色餐饮。建筑特色明显，层层退台式建筑成为临江最亮丽的风景线。

Heyi Avenue: A high-end shopping center that gathers international top-tier brands. It features a wide array of renowned international brands and a variety of specialty dining options. The architecture of this commercial complex is distinctive, and its terraced design renders it the most stunning city skyline of the nearby riverside buildings.

宁波阪急百货——日本阪急阪神在中国大陆的第一家分店。集聚众多一线奢侈品品牌、国际潮奢品牌、国际美妆品牌，其中100余个为宁波首店品牌。阪急百货还汇集了近80家特色餐饮品牌，是宁波新晋网红商场，也是宁波最具时尚度的消费场所。

和义大道　Heyi Avenue

宁波阪急百货　Hankyu Department Store in Ningbo

Hankyu Department Store: The first branch of Japan's Hankyu Hanshin in Chinese mainland. It is home to numerous first-line luxury brands, international luxury fashion boutiques and international beauty brands, of which more than 100 make their first appearance in Ningbo. Ningbo Hankyu – also gathering nearly 80 specialty food and beverage brands – is a rising internet-famous shopping mall and the most trendy consumption spot across the city.

鄞州万达广场——宁波鄞州中心区最早的大型综合体商场。一家集购物、餐饮、娱乐、休闲于一体的综合性购物中心，拥有丰富的商业资源和完善的服务体系。

Yinzhou Wanda Plaza: The earliest large-scale shopping complex in the center of Yinzhou, Ningbo. It is a comprehensive shopping center integrating shopping, dining, entertainment and leisure.

万象城——宁波第一家拥有摩天轮主题区的商场。汇聚400余个品牌，包括FOODHALL食品主题区、THINKSPACE儿童主题区、幸运摩天轮三大

鄞州万达广场　Yinzhou Wanda Plaza

万象城　MixC Ningbo

特色区域。

MixC Ningbo: The first shopping mall in Ningbo featuring a Ferris Wheel-themed area. The retail development brings together more than 400 brands and covers three special areas: the food theme area of FOODHALL, the children's theme area of THINKSPACE, and the lucky Ferris Wheel.

宁波来福士广场——新加坡凯德置地在宁波的首个综合商业项目。入驻200多个优秀品牌，涵盖国际潮牌、时尚饰品、特色餐饮、新型娱乐、影城等丰富业态，深受年轻客群的喜爱。

Raffles City: CapitaLand Singapore's first mixed-use commercial project in Ningbo. As a favorite among the younger clientele, this city landmark commercial harbors over 200 famous brands, encompassing international trendy brands, fashionable accessories, specialty dining, modern entertainment, and cinemas.

宁波来福士广场　Raffles City

杉井奥特莱斯——宁波最大的以奥莱业态为特色的商业综合体。聚集超过 260 个国内外品牌，随着超级大店、城市旗舰店、浙东首店等相继落地，杉井奥特莱斯成为“长三角消费打卡地”。

Shanjing Outlets: Ningbo's largest commercial complex featuring the outlet business. Here more than 260 domestic and international brands, super large stores, city flagship stores, and the first stores of their kind in East Zhejiang have landed one after another. Shanjing Outlets has become a popular destination for consumers in the Yangtze River Delta Region.

K11 艺术购物中心——香港新世界打造的浙江省首家 K11 艺术商业中心（在建）。打破商业、产业、艺术、文化的边界，是集特色文化、艺术资源于一体的社交型商业空间。

THE PARK by K11 Select: The first K11 art mall in Zhejiang Province (under construction). This art mall built by Hong Kong New World makes a social

杉井奥特莱斯　Shanjing Outlets

business space integrating special cultural and artistic resources, breaking the boundaries of art, culture, commerce, and industry.

（二）特色街区
Featured Neighborhoods

宁波街巷众多，各具特色，形成了现代商业街区、休闲娱乐街区、风味食品街区、民间特色街区、历史文化街区等特色街区。这些街区既保留着几百年的历史底蕴，又紧跟现代商业趋势，呈现出一种独特的魅力和活力。

Ningbo is home to diversified streets and alleys that create vibrant neighborhoods characterized by modern commerce, leisure and entertainment, flavorful food, local flair, and historical culture. These neighborhoods exhibit a unique charm and vitality, not only preserving centuries of historical essence but also keeping pace with modern commercial trends.

老外滩——宁波最具中外风情的商业街区。获评国家级旅游休闲街区、国家级示范步行街，位于宁波市核心区域——三江口北岸，是浙江省唯一现存的能反映中国近代港口文化的外滩，是百年宁波的重要见证地。天主教堂、酒吧一条街、夜景、三江夜游共同体现了老外滩的独特魅力。

The Old Bund (Laowaitan): Ningbo's com-mercial district rich in both Chinese and foreign charm. This is named both as a national tourism and leisure block and a national model pedestrian street. Located in the heart of Ningbo city – the north bank of Sanjiangkou, it is the only existing waterfront in Zhejiang Province and showcases the culture of modern Chinese ports while providing a significant

老外滩 The Old Bund (Laowaitan)

testament to the history of the port city. The distinctive allure of the Old Bund is beautifully encapsulated by its Catholic church, bar street, nighttime scenery, and the Three Rivers night cruise.

南塘老街——展现宁波江南水乡特征的历史商业街区。国家级旅游休闲街区，集历史古迹、旅游观光、文化休闲、宁波老字号、宁波名优特产、民俗特色于一体，是体验宁波味道的不二之选。

Nantang Old Street: A historical commercial area characteristic of a Jiangnan water town in Ningbo. This national-level tourism and leisure block blends historical landmarks, tourist attractions, cultural leisure, time-honored Ningbo

南塘老街　Nantang Old Street

鼓楼步行街　Gulou Pedestrian Street

brands, renowned local specialties, and folk customs. It is a must-see destination for tourists to savor the flavors of Ningbo.

鼓楼步行街——最具宁波历史文化底蕴的商业街。宁波乃至浙江省的标志性步行街，有着古老的建筑、丰富的传统手工艺品和特色小吃，体现了宁波独特的历史底蕴和地域风情。

Gulou Pedestrian Street: The commercial street with the richest historical and cultural heritage of Ningbo. It is a landmark pedestrian street in Ningbo and across Zhejiang Province. This area preserves ancient buildings, rich traditional handicrafts and specialty snacks, embracing Ningbo's unique historical heritage and regional flavor.

水街——独具夜间文化特色的时尚街区。第三批省级夜间文化和旅游消费集聚区，打造了“鄞州之夜”“宁波爵士生活节”“南商有好物”三大城市级年轻力 IP，成为宁波年轻力夜间文旅经济的引领者。

Shui Street (Water Street)—A fashionable nighttime block. It was included in the third batch of provincial-level nighttime cultural and tourism consumption clusters. By creating three major city-level youth IPs ("Yinzhou Night", "Ningbo Jazz Life Festival", and "Nanshang's Goodies"), this block has emerged as the epicenter of Ningbo's vibrant nightlife and cultural tourism economy.

溪口民国风情街——宁波最具民国风情的商业街区。总建筑面积 15 万平方米，是以“民国风情＋蒋氏文化＋溪口地域文化”为主题，覆盖全年龄段的复合型家庭娱乐休闲购物体验新景区。

Xikou Republican Style Street: Ningbo's most Republican-style commercial neighborhood. It is located in Xikou Town, Fenghua District, with a total construction area of 150000 square meters. This new scenic spot features composite

水街 Shui Street (Water Street)

溪口民国风情街　Xikou Republican Style Street

family entertainment, leisure and shopping experience, covering all ages with the theme of "Republic of China style + Chiang's culture + Xikou's regional culture".

（三）专业市场
Specialized Markets

宁波不仅拥有服装市场、海鲜市场、茶叶市场等独具当地特色的专业市场，也有众多国际化特色市场，在这里你能获得更经济实惠、更便捷高效、更具市井气息的购物体验。

Ningbo boasts local specialty markets in clothing, seafood, and tea, as well as international-style specialized markets, where you can experience a more affordable, convenient and efficient shopping experience with a more urban flavor.

中东欧国家特色商品常年馆——宁波最具中东欧特色的购物场所。一期由综合馆、国别商品馆、专业品牌馆三种类型的场馆组成，以商品展示和交易为主；二期由主题展示区、经贸活动区和功能配套区组成。总规模 3.2 万平方米，集聚中东欧贸易企业 50 余家，不同特色商品馆 34 个，常年展示酒类、食品、美妆个护、工艺品、日用品等近 5000 个单品。

The CEEC Products Permanent Pavilion: Ningbo's shopping destination with the most distinctive CEEC flair. Phase One of this pavilion, consisting of three sub-types of pavilions such as the Comprehensive Pavilion, the CEEC Commodity Pavilion, and the Specialized Brand Pavilion, focuses on the display and trading of commodities. The second phase is composed of a thematic exhibition area, a business and trade activity area, and a functional support area, featuring facilities to create interactive and immersive consumption experiences for visitors. The total area of the pavilion has now increased to 32000 m^2 and the number of exhibition halls to 34. There are nearly 5000 products displayed, including wine, food, cosmetics, handiworks, and daily necessities, from CEECs throughout the year.

中东欧国家特色商品常年馆 The CEEC Products Permanent Pavilion

致　谢

在宁波市委组织部的指导和支持下，《世界的宁波，宁波的世界》城市引才主题图书编写工作从2023年开始启动，编写组从宁波经济发展、产业人才、自然风光、民俗文化、商业生活等多个视角进行了探索，力求全方位展现宁波现代化滨海大都市的城市形象，帮助世界各地人才快速了解宁波、走进宁波。

在主题图书编写过程中，编写组还得到了宁波人才发展集团李雪然、黄鑫、冯彬、王松杰、赵颖琦、施佳秀、雷小慧、汪润明、吴扶生、俞奕戎、王莹、董恺煊、刘思莹、王思文、文传旭、钱成光、沈建锋、陈新月、朱景行、刘巧敏、邱佳宁、孙一婷、张心怡以及摄影师龚国荣、唐严、徐能、严龙、郑凯侠、蒋晓东、卓松磊、范洪、忻之承、许天长、丁峰、樊建威、胡龙召的鼎力支持。在此，对他们表示衷心的感谢！

Acknowledgements

We express our sincere gratitude to the Organization Department of the CPC Ningbo Municipal Committee for their guidance and assistance in initiating the themed book *Ningbo, A Coastal City for Global Minds* in 2023. Our dedicated compilation group explored various aspects of Ningbo, including its economic development, industrial talents, natural scenery, folk culture, and commercial life, from multiple perspectives. Our aim was to showcase Ningbo as a modern coastal metropolis and facilitate a quick and comprehensive understanding of the city for talents from around the world.

During the compilation process, we received generous support from the staff of Ningbo Talent Development Group, including Li Xueran, Huang Xin, Feng Bin, Wang Songjie, Zhao Yingqi, Shi Jiaxiu, Lei Xiaohui, Wang Runming, Wu Fusheng, Yu Yirong, Wang Ying, Dong Kaixuan, Liu Siying, Wang Siwen, Wen Chuanxu, Qian Chengguang, Shen Jianfeng, Chen Xinyue, Zhu Jingxing, Liu Qiaomin, Qiu Jianing, Sun Yiting and Zhang Xinyi. We are also grateful to the photographers, Gong Guorong, Tang Yan, Xu Neng, Yan Long, Zheng Kaixia, Jiang Xiaodong, Zhuo Songlei, Fan Hong, Xin Zhicheng, Xu Tianchang, Ding Feng, Fan Jianwei, and Hu Longzhao, for their valuable contributions. We would like to express our heartfelt thanks to everyone involved in this project. Your support and hard work were instrumental in the successful completion of this book.